D0406416

SPELL IT RIGHT!

HARRY SHAW

THIRD EDITION

SPELL IT RIGHT!

PERENNIAL LIBRARY

HARPER & ROW, PUBLISHERS, NEW YORK
CAMBRIDGE, PHILADELPHIA, SAN FRANCISCO
WASHINGTON, LONDON, MEXICO CITY
SÃO PAULO, SINGAPORE, SYDNEY

SPELL IT RIGHT! (*Third Edition*). Copyright © 1961, 1965, 1986 by Harry Shaw. All rights reserved. Printed in the United States of America. No part of this book may be used or reproduced in any manner whatsoever without written permission except in the case of brief quotations embodied in critical articles and reviews. For information address Harper & Row, Publishers, Inc., 10 East 53rd Street, New York, N.Y. 10022. Published simultaneously in Canada by Fitzhenry & Whiteside Limited, Toronto.

First PERENNIAL LIBRARY edition published 1986.

Library of Congress Cataloging-in-Publication Data

Shaw, Harry, 1905–
  Spell it right!

  "Perennial Library."
  Includes index.
  1. English language—Orthography and spelling.
I. Title.
PE1143.S48 1986   428.1   85-45920
ISBN 0-06-097048-0 (pbk.)

87 88 89 90 MP 10 9 8 7 6 5 4 3 2

FOR JANE BAYARD WILSON SHAW
WHO, THROUGH LOVE AND KNOWLEDGE,
FOSTERED THE LIFELONG INTEREST OF
HER SON IN THE SUBJECT OF SPELLING

CONTENTS

FOREWORD   *xi*

1. YOU AND THE PROBLEM
   OF SPELLING   *1*

   Why Correct Spelling Is Important   *1*
   Why Spelling Is Difficult   *3*
   A Brief History of English Spelling   *4*
   Some Comforting Thoughts About Spelling   *8*

2. TACKLING THE PROBLEM   *12*

   Forming Mental Images   *13*
   Auditory Images   *13*
   Motor Images   *13*
   Six Paths to Correct Spelling   *14*

3. ACTUALLY SEE WORDS AS
   WELL AS HEAR THEM   *16*

   Your Perception Span   *17*
   How to "See" Words Mentally   *18*
   Look-Alikes and Sound-Alikes   *19*

4. PRONOUNCE WORDS
   CAREFULLY AND CORRECTLY   *43*

   Dictionary Sound Systems   *44*
   Words Confused in Pronunciation   *46*
   Incorrect Prefixes   *47*
   Added Vowels   *48*
   Dropped Vowels   *48*
   Dropped Consonants   *50*
   Unstressed Vowels   *51*
   Silent Letters   *53*

5. USE A DICTIONARY:
   ETYMOLOGY   56

   The Dictionary As an Aid in Spelling   56
   Choice of a Dictionary   57
   Word Derivation and Spelling   57

6. USE A DICTIONARY:
   PREFIXES, SUFFIXES, AND
   COMBINING FORMS   61

   Prefixes   62
   Suffixes   65
   Combining Forms   78

7. USE A DICTIONARY: PLURALS   81

   Noun Plurals   81
   Compound Nouns   83
   Irregular Plurals   84
   Nouns of Foreign Origin   84

8. USE A DICTIONARY:
   APOSTROPHES   86

   Indicating Possession   86
   Indicating Omission   87
   Forming Plurals   87

9. USE A DICTIONARY:
   COMPOUND WORDS   90

   Principles of Word Joining   90
   Seven Classes of Compound Words   91
   General Cautions in Using the Hyphen   94

10. USE A DICTIONARY:
    CAPITALIZATION   96

    The Conventions of Capital Letters   96
    Capitalizing First Words   96
    Capitalizing Proper Nouns   97
    Capitals in Poetry and in Titles   98
    The Careless Use of Capital Letters   98

11. LEARN A FEW SIMPLE RULES OF SPELLING *101*

The *EI-IE* Rule *102*
The Final *Y* Rule *104*
The Final *E* Rule *105*
The Inserted *K* Rule *107*
The Final Consonant Rule *107*
The "One Plus One" Rule *109*

12. SPELL CAREFULLY *111*

Carelessness and Haste *111*
Proofreading *112*
Vision Spread *113*

13. USE MEMORY DEVICES *117*

Mnemonics As a Spelling Aid *118*
Memory Clues to Selected
Troublesome Words *119*

14. LISTING MISSPELLED WORDS *122*

The Value of Spelling Lists *122*
The Twenty Most Often Misspelled Words *123*
List of 860 Words Often Misspelled *125*

15. TWENTY-FIVE TROUBLESOME BEGINNINGS AND ENDINGS *138*

16. TEST YOURSELF: THIRTY-FIVE GAMES AND QUIZZES *147*

GLOSSARY: TERMS USED IN THIS BOOK *161*

INDEX *169*

FOREWORD

Correct spelling is essential for intelligent communication. It is taken for granted and expected at all times. Yet many people realize their writing sometimes contains spelling errors, and they are embarrassed by doubts and fears about the correct spelling of difficult words. Distraction, confusion, and misunderstanding result from errors in spelling. Therefore, no one should be satisfied with anything less than perfection.

Perhaps you are one of those people who feel disturbed by their spelling errors and have enough of a spelling conscience to do something about it. Or perhaps you are among those who doubt their ability to master this difficult subject. You may have tried many times and failed. If so, is there any hope for you?

The answer is that if you really have a desire to learn to spell perfectly you can, provided:

1. You can pronounce such words as *accept* and *except* so that they will not sound exactly alike.
2. You can look at such words as *sad* and *sand* and in a single glance, without moving your eyes, detect the difference between them.
3. You can sign your name without looking at the paper on which you are writing and without even consciously thinking about what you are doing.
4. You can tell your friend Bill from your friend Sam by a mere glance.
5. You can learn a simple rhyme, such as "Old King Cole was a merry old soul . . ."
6. You can remember that a compl*i*ment is "what *I* like to get."
7. You can learn the alphabet, if you do not know it already.
8. You can equip yourself with a reliable desk dictionary.

9. You can learn what a syllable is and proofread your writing syllable-by-syllable.
10. You have normal intelligence, here defined as the ability to read and write simple English and keep out of the way of speeding automobiles.

If you can honestly meet these ten provisions, you can learn to spell *without ever making a mistake.* If you can pass Number 10 and only three or four of the others, you can still double your spelling efficiency. It's worth trying, isn't it?

The approaches and attacks are all included in the chapters which follow. If you just cannot wait to start, skip to Chapter 2 and begin there. If you lose heart, turn back to the first chapter. It can be very helpful, too.

Wherever you start, start NOW.

SPELL IT RIGHT!

YOU AND THE PROBLEM OF SPELLING

The one thing demanded of those who have had educational advantages is that they be able to spell. In your daily work or in social situations you may not need to be able to add a column of figures. Few people will care. Not often will you be thought stupid if you don't know the dates of historical events—say, the Battle of Waterloo. Your knowledge of economics can be nil. You may not know the difference between an oboe and an ibis, an atom and a molecule. But if you can't spell, you're in trouble. Rightly or wrongly, fairly or unfairly, misspelling is the most frequently accepted sign of illiteracy.

Why is this? You can argue that the ability to think clearly is far more important than spelling. So are clear expression of thoughts, an attractive personality, and demonstrated ability in one's job. The fact remains that incorrect spelling is heavily penalized in our society—so heavily that it keeps people from getting jobs they want or prevents them from moving up to better positions. Inability to spell gives people complexes just as much as unsureness about grammar or proper methods of dress and social behavior.

WHY CORRECT SPELLING IS IMPORTANT

Job opportunities are missed and employees are often let go because of spelling deficiencies. Even business enterprises can suffer because of their inability to meet commonly accepted spelling practices. In an eastern city a store was opened for the sale of Army surplus goods: canteens, combat boots, pup tents, plastic boxes, and various other items. Over the door was a sign that said COME IN AND BROUSE AROUND. One day somebody told the owner that BROUSE was a misspelling. So he had it painted this way: COME IN AND BROWZE AROUND. Another customer complained and the owner got another repainting: COME IN AND BROWS AROUND. There must have been more complaints, because a few days later a new sign appeared which

read: COME IN AND BROUSE, BROWZE OR BROWS AROUND—BUT
COME IN. A month or so later, the owner tacked up another sign
over that one. It read: GOING OUT OF BIZNESS.

The main reason for reliance on spelling as an index of intelligence and literacy is that correct spelling is the one fixed and certain
thing about our language. The overwhelming majority of English
words are spelled in only one way; all other ways are wrong. The
accepted system *is* accepted. It is the system in which our business
communications, our magazines, our newspapers, and our books have
been written for generations.

This uniformity applies to no other aspect of our language. You
can vary your choice of words as much as you please. You can write
sentences which are long or short and punctuate them in various
ways. In most circles you can split an infinitive or use a double
negative and not be penalized. But you can spell a word in only one
correct way. In a rapidly changing world this substantial uniformity
is understandably attractive to many people, particularly to those
who are good spellers.

Even where alternative spellings are possible, only one will be
thought correct for a given piece of writing. For example, both *telephone* and *phone* are commonly used, the latter a colloquial form of
telephone. Your employer may insist on *telephone,* and that full spelling
will then be the right one. Both *theater* and *theatre* are correct spellings, but you would probably use the former in the United States
and the latter in England.

One might argue logically that many wrong spellings are "better"
than the right ones since they "show" the word more clearly. *Wensday*
more clearly reveals the sound of the word than does *Wednesday.*
But logic and common sense will not help; in Old English *Wödnes
daeg* was the day of the god Woden, and the *d* has remained. Spelling
is frequently a matter of conforming not to logic but to custom and
tradition.

If enough people make a "mistake" in punctuation, or grammar,
or the meaning of a word, that "mistake" becomes acceptable usage.
This is a scientific fact of language. Through the years our language
has changed, and will change, in its idioms, its vocabulary, its pronunciation, and its structural form. Change is the essential, inevitable
phenomenon of a living language, as it is of any living organism. But

this observation, this law, does not yet apply to the spelling of English words.

For many generations, spelling practice has been supported by sentiment, convention, prejudice, and custom. This is strong support, since each of us can think of many other activities similarly reinforced. The world is largely ruled by sentiment. A hundred, a thousand, observances are based only upon convention. Think briefly of the clothes people wear, table manners, office etiquette, and you will see the point. If sentiment, convention, and custom were removed from our social order, our way of living would be altered beyond recognition.

If English spelling were much more illogical than it is, the problem might be solved. Then no one could spell correctly; all of us would be bad spellers together. But enough people have learned to spell correctly to make things difficult for those who can't. This is the situation today, and we must make the best of it.

At some time in the distant future, correct spelling may be thought unimportant. Until that time, we can take comfort in realizing that spelling, like every other activity of the human mind, *can* be learned. It will have to be if we are to free ourselves from the doubts and frustrations which diminish our self-confidence when we write. It will have to be if we wish to "get ahead," to be socially acceptable, to be considered educated and literate.

WHY SPELLING IS DIFFICULT

Correct spelling is so important for social and business reasons that we feel obligated to learn to spell as well as we can, perfectly if possible. The task is not simple. It would be easier if spelling were always logical and consistent. But from bitter experience we know that the spelling of English words is illogical and inconsistent. In fact, it is downright eccentric and, on occasion, idiotic—as writers through the years have gleefully, or wrathfully, pointed out. Thorstein Veblen, famed author of *The Theory of the Leisure Class,* once wrote that English spelling satisfies all the requirements "of conspicuous waste. It is archaic, cumbrous, and ineffective . . . failure to acquire it is easy of detection . . ." as many of us know to our sorrow. And former President Andrew Jackson once angrily commented that it is a poor mind which cannot think of more than one way to spell a word.

Why is spelling difficult? The primary reason is that the correct spelling of many words does not even approximate the sounds being represented. Our speech has steadily drifted away from traditional writing and the process is continuing. Because our language is constantly changing, it is likely that spelling will tend to differ more and more from pronunciation. Unless spelling undergoes reform (and strong opposition has always prevented this) our spelling may proceed to the point where many words become ideographic. This means that a written symbol (a spelled word) will represent something directly rather than stand for the actual sound of the word itself. This tendency—exemplified by the contrasting pronunciation and spelling of such words as *cough, Worcester,* and *knife*—has been evident for centuries. Some experts believe that this difference will become greater and greater.

Not only are numerous words not spelled as they sound, but many which sound alike are spelled differently. Any system is suspect which tolerates *fine* and *sign.* We have identical pronunciations for *no* and *know; cite, sight*, and *site* sound alike. No one unfamiliar with English and English spelling would ever imagine that *kernel* and *colonel* have the same sound.

A BRIEF HISTORY OF ENGLISH SPELLING

No adequate history of English spelling has ever been written, and certainly this small book is not the place to attempt one. But a brief review of known facts about our language will help to account for some of the admitted difficulties of English spelling.

For about one thousand years before the Christian era, our linguistic ancestors were semi-savages wandering through northern Europe. These tribes consisted of Angles, Saxons, and Jutes and spoke several dialects of what is known as Low German, or *Plattdeutsch.* They had some contact with the Roman Empire and promptly began a process which has continued unabated to the present day: they started borrowing words from Latin and placing them in their own vocabularies. We still use many everyday words borrowed by these tribes: *bishop, butter, cheap, cheese, church, plum, kettle, street,* etc.

When the Roman Empire began to weaken, it had to give up its occupancy of what we now know as England, and the Germanic tribes, commonly called Anglo-Saxons, began to move in. We know little about the arrival of the Anglo-Saxons in England in the fifth century A.D., but we do know that after the year 600 they were converted to Christianity and that borrowing from Latin became even more pronounced. To what was then Anglo-Saxon, or Old English, were added many words which are in use today, such as *alms, anthem, martyr, palm,* and *priest.*

England even then was considered an attractive place, and Norsemen from Denmark and the Scandinavian peninsula began a long series of hit-and-run raids. Forays of the Norsemen continued until the eleventh century, with the linguistic result that many Norse words were added to the language. Examples are *crawl, egg, law, race, scowl,* and *tree.* Even our pronouns *they, them,* and *their* are of Norse origin. So is our suffix *-by,* the Danish word for "farm" or "town," which appears in so many place names, such as *Derby.*

Another event of great importance to our language (and spelling) was the Norman Conquest. The Normans, originally from Scandinavia, settled in northern France in the tenth century and adopted the French language. In 1066 they crossed the English Channel and became the masters of England. French became the language of the nobility, the court, and polite society, although the common people continued to use English. Our language was profoundly affected by the introduction of French; literally thousands of words were added to the English vocabulary between 1100 and 1500. A few examples will serve to show this borrowing: *bacon, baptism, biscuit, blanket, bucket, chess, curtain, fault, flower, government, grammar, incense, lamp, lemon, logic, parson, religion, scarlet, surprise, towel.*

Beginning about 1500, the discovery of new lands brought many thousands of other new words to the English language. Words from such remote regions as India, China, Africa, and North America enriched the language tremendously. Among familiar words borrowed, for example, from the North American Indians may be mentioned *Connecticut, Massachusetts, Monongahela, squaw, tomahawk,* and *wampum.*

In short, during the past thousand years our language has far more than doubled its size. Words have come pouring into the language from French, Latin, Greek, Hebrew, Arabic, and a score of other tongues. Many of these words are difficult to spell, at least in part because of their pronunciation.

This brief comment on English is grossly inadequate as linguistic history, but its purpose is to make clear one dominant reason why spelling and pronunciation are so far apart. When these many thousands of words first arrived in English they often appeared with the spellings, or phonetic (sound) approximations of the spellings, which they originally had and which did not always conform to the customs of English. Sometimes, the spellings of words were modified to conform to the English tongue; many times they were not. The English language is a linguistic grab bag with tremendous range and flexibility. Unfortunately, its very richness compounds our spelling problems.

English is indeed a polyglot language, but that is not all. Present-day spelling often reflects pronunciations of several centuries ago. Between the time of Chaucer (1340–1400) and Shakespeare (1564–1616) our language underwent changes in pronunciation which contributed to the chaos of modern spelling.

For example, in Chaucer's time *mouse* sounded like our *moose; moon* resembled our pronunciation of *moan*. These shifts in vowel sounds (as well as in others) were thorough. However, since we have retained some of the Chaucerian (Middle English) system of spelling, Modern and Chaucerian English seem closer than they really are. Genuine differences are hidden by our spelling system.

Another change during this period from Chaucer to Shakespeare was the complete elimination of a vowel sound in certain positions. Chaucer pronounced *name* and *dance* as two syllables. Shakespeare pronounced them as one, as do we. Similarly, Chaucer pronounced the word *laughed* as two syllables: laugh-ed, but of course we do not. This elimination of a vowel sound affected hundreds of quite common words and gave a different aspect to the language. The "silent" vowel in English is responsible for as many misspellings as any other one cause (it will be discussed in Chapter 4).

These two changes in pronunciation (but not in spelling) account for some of the basic differences between the English of Chaucer's time and that of today. Furthermore, a number of other sound changes have occurred since the time of Shakespeare and are still going on. People in the sixteenth and seventeenth centuries, for example, pronounced *reason* as we do *raisin*. They also sounded the *l* in a word like *palm.* Our pronunciation has changed, but our spelling has not—with consequent grief for all poor spellers.

Why is it that pronunciation is ever changing and spelling is not? Many reasons can be cited, but two are outstanding.

First, standardization of spelling is due more to the invention of printing than to any other single cause. Prior to the introduction of printing into England by William Caxton in 1475, most people were not concerned with spelling. Reading and writing were activities carried on only by monks and other learned men. So long as people communicated solely by speech, spelling was no problem. But when printing came in, some standards had to be set up; otherwise, chaos would have resulted because those who read would have been utterly confused by whimsically varied spelling. As larger and larger numbers of people began to read and write, they saw and used the standardized spellings employed by scholars, "editors," and printers. These standards were loose and flexible, to be sure, but they represented a forward step in communication. This unification of the language, though partial and imperfect, had a profound effect on writing but not, of course, on speech.

Second, a major regulatory and controlling influence on the language came from early dictionary-makers. The first English dictionary in 1603 spelled and briefly defined a little more than two thousand words. Its compiler did what his predecessors had done when translating Latin words into English: he copied. Naturally, on numerous occasions he imitated the spellings of his predecessors and thus tended to freeze them.

This earliest dictionary was imitated, or expanded upon, by several other lexicographers. In 1755, Dr. Samuel Johnson published his famous dictionary, a serious, important work which has influenced all lexicographers ever since. His dictionary dominated—and tended to fix—English spelling and usage for more than a century.

In the United States the great pioneer in dictionary-making was Noah Webster. His first work, published in 1806, advocated spelling *head* as *hed* and *thumb* as *thum,* but his efforts at spelling reform were generally rejected by the public. In other respects, however, his work was widely accepted; and in 1828 his *An American Dictionary of the English Language* began to exert its lasting influence on English in this country. Lexicographers since Webster have been somewhat more reliable than he in reporting actual usage but they, too, have had to report spelling as it is found in printed sources. Thus, spelling has become fixed and largely unchangeable, although it frequently does not represent actual pronunciation and often departs from common sense.

SOME COMFORTING THOUGHTS
ABOUT SPELLING

If you have read this far, you may have become discouraged about ever learning to spell correctly. You may say, and with reason, that such a weird and illogical system deserves not study but contempt. Nevertheless, you know from experience that powerful social and business considerations force you to master the subject. Actually, the problem is not so difficult to solve as it may seem.

In the first place, psychologists and experienced educators have proved over and over again that any person of normal intelligence can learn to spell. Like any other activity of the human mind, spelling can be approached, grasped, and mastered. It is easier for some people to spell correctly than it is for others. This is understandable; some people can master calculus or ice-skating or sewing or typing or reading more easily than others. Spelling correctly may not be simple for you, but it surely cannot be termed impossible. Hundreds of thousands of "bad" spellers have conquered their difficulties. So can you, if you really desire to and will apply yourself to the task. No special quality of mind, no rare set of mental or motor reflexes, is involved.

It is true, however, that minds work in different ways. The best and easiest way for John or Mary to learn to spell correctly may not be the most efficient for George or Abigail. But one or more of the six approaches discussed in this book will help John, Mary, George, Abigail—and you. What you need is the will, the desire, to learn. Having that, and normal intelligence, you are fully equipped. One commentator on spelling has flatly stated: "All the investigations indicate that any *child* of normal intelligence can learn to spell with very little difficulty in a reasonable length of time."

A second comforting thought about spelling is that probably only a few words cause most of the trouble. Learning to spell may seem a hopeless task because so many thousands of words must be mastered. But remember that no one is expected to be able to spell every word on demand. A physician might be able to spell *sphyg-momanometer*, but nearly everyone else would have to look it up in a dictionary. And since physicians are no better spellers than any other group of educated people, they, like us, would properly consult a dictionary when writing such "demons" as *piccalilli, platyrrhine,* and *pseudepigrapha.* (These words may seem strange because many of us have never used them in our entire lives. Yet each appears in standard desk dictionaries.)

We use remarkably few different words in ordinary speech, and the overwhelming majority of them cause no problems whatever. It may be both startling and reassuring to learn that only twelve simple words account for about 25 percent of everything spoken and written in English. The dozen most used words in English are *a, and, he, I, in, it, is, of, that, the, to,* and *was.* These twelve and thirty-eight more (a total of fifty words) make up half of the running total in all English speech and writing. If you increase the number to the thousand most common words in English, you will account for 80 percent of all words everyone uses in speaking and writing and comes across in reading.

You may be inclined to doubt these statements, but they are substantiated by the word count contained in *The Teacher's Word Book of 30,000 Words,* prepared under the direction of two outstanding scholars, Edward L. Thorndike and Irving Lorge (New York: Teachers College, 1944). Other experts unhesitatingly accept the findings of Thorndike and Lorge.

If only one thousand different words appear in some 80 percent of all the expressions that one says, hears, writes, and reads, it follows that the task of learning to spell that small number should be simple. And yet the problem is even more elementary: almost none of the thousand words creates any spelling difficulty whatever for the ordinary writer.

In a running count of many millions of words used by speakers and writers of English, the words *a, and, of, the,* and *to* will appear more than a hundred thousand times; *he, I, in, it, is, that,* and *was* will appear more than fifty thousand times. None of these words is a spelling demon, nor indeed are many of the 620 words appearing more than one thousand times in the same word count. For proof of this statement, note the thirty-nine most often used words beginning with the letter *a:*

a	all	answer
about	almost	any
according	alone	anything
across	along	appear
act	already	are
action	also	arm
add	always	army
after	am	around
afternoon	American	art
again	among	as
against	an	ask
age	and	at
ago	another	away

Do you find any hard-to-spell words in this list? And just so that you will not think the list is rigged with words starting with *a*, see whether the *u* words are any more difficult:

uncle	United States	upon
under	until	us
understand	up	use

You can come to terms with the spelling problem if you will narrow your sights and concentrate on the few, but very real, troublemakers. When driving a car haven't you often noticed in the distance a hill which looked very steep, the road up it almost vertical? As you got closer, the road seemed to smooth out, didn't it? What seemed an impossibly sharp climb became a simple grade. Learning to spell involves climbing a grade, but not a very steep one, once you get close to the problem.

Another reassuring thought about learning to spell is that the task can become good fun and provide much pleasure. This statement may seem absurd, but it is an acknowledged fact of human behavior that the more proficient a person becomes in some activity, the greater his pleasure in it. Ever watch a figure skater? Two boys with a baseball? A woman knitting? A mother giving her child a bath? Two chess players? Someone lost in a book?

Learning to spell involves discipline, concentration, and some hard work. But so do figure-skating, baseball, knitting, and reading. Proficiency provides pleasure in these activities; often the more skill attained, the greater the pleasure. Further, most activities can best be learned by actually participating in them, not just memorizing rules or reading about them in books or magazines.

After you have attained greater proficiency in spelling by following the suggestions in this book, you will find word games enjoyable. Crossword puzzles and cryptograms are not recommended for the initial phases of spelling study. Yet they can, and do, provide pleasure for many people and unquestionably increase one's basic vocabulary and spelling proficiency. Many average spellers have become excellent ones through games like Scrabble and anagrams. Only a few decades ago, spelling bees were commonly held in almost every grade school in the country. They provided fun and excitement for those who participated, as some of my readers can testify. National spelling bees are still an annual occurrence. Perhaps some television program will revive the old-time spelling bee, with pleasure and profit for contestants and viewers.

Recently, my wife and I had dinner with another couple. After returning to the living room, our host suggested that instead of playing bridge or engaging in small talk, we try a spelling game. Each of us wrote down on paper three words which we thought would cause spelling difficulties for the others. We read out our lists in turn and the others wrote them down. When each of us had written the twelve words, we read out the spellings and settled arguments by using a dictionary. Result: we added some new words to our vocabularies, fixed their spellings in mind, and enjoyed ourselves immensely. You might like to know a few of the "demons" used that night. Here they are: *picnicking, phthisic, deciduous, gnat, medieval, ptomaine, dahlia, garrulous, tendency, picayune, ecstasy, liquefy, battalion, dilemma, obsession, amoeba, iridescent, supercilious.*

Several of these words are of little practical value. That's not the point. What is important is that four people of ordinary intelligence derived pleasure and profit from a "dull" spelling game.

Learning to spell well is not a matter of tricks and mirrors; it is not a dull and dreary chore; it is not an unending task which stretches out indefinitely. It is a subject which can be mastered with some effort and imagination—and a common-sense approach.

2

TACKLING THE PROBLEM

Nearly every spelling authority who has written on the subject has presented some sure-fire approach to the problem of poor spelling. All other methods are wrong; his is the only true one. And his method *has* worked—for some people. For others it has been a flat failure. There was nothing especially wrong with his method except that it did not allow for the fact that people differ. They differ in sex, color, and personality—and they differ in ways of learning. The system by which A learns easily and quickly may work poorly for B or may not work at all. There is no one guaranteed method for everyone, but some plans for studying spelling are sounder than others. Actually, spelling is sometimes "taught" in such a fashion as to preclude any possibility of real success. Before explaining the six approaches recommended in this book, we should review a few facts about people and the learning process.

Our minds operate in accordance with certain principles. We may call them *laws* if we wish, although reputable experimental psychologists would hardly do so. For instance, you have probably long since found out that you can remember something which is important to you. You can remember it so well, so clearly, that you think you could never forget it. You also realize that you can conveniently fail to remember things you wish to forget—dental appointments, for example.

Incentive, then, or a strong motive to remember, will facilitate memory. And a good memory will aid the process of learning. Thus, the task of learning to spell will come easier to you if you bear in mind the practical value to be gained and discipline yourself to study and practice.

FORMING MENTAL IMAGES

The mental process most important in word study is the ability to form mental pictures, or *mental images* as they may be called. These images are of several types. For example, each of us can form some sort of visual image when a suggested idea calls up in our minds a picture. When the word *church* is suggested to you, you immediately "see in your mind" a picture of the object named. So do I, although your visual image and mine may differ. Almost any object—automobile, child, office manager, snow—will summon up for you, and for everyone, some sort of visual image.

This power of visualization is far stronger in some people than in others. You may know every detail about your bedroom and yet not be able to see it in your mind's eye. Many of us have lapses in our powers of visualization. Therefore, the suggestion set forth later, that you "mentally see" words, may or may not be helpful to you. If it isn't, some other approach will make more sense. It's no discredit not to have visual memory, although it is true that this mental process can be trained. You probably can close your eyes and, without difficulty, see your own signature. But you may not be able to "see" any of the words you persistently misspell. If so, try another approach.

AUDITORY IMAGES

When a suggested idea summons up a memory of what the object sounds like, we have an *auditory* (hearing) image. Some of us can, and some cannot, "mentally hear" the sounds named in "the bark of a gun," "the popping of hot fat," "the song of a lark," "the laughter of children." Being auditory-minded is not especially helpful in learning to spell, unless we are also visual-minded. If we are both, the sounds of a few words can be compared with their visual images. Some of the memory devices (*mnemonics*) suggested later (Chapter 13) depend upon this relationship.

MOTOR IMAGES

Related to the visual image and the auditory image is the *motor* image. Motor images are connected with the use of different muscles in the body. If you are a swimmer and think of the last lap in a long race, you can summon up the feeling of weary arm and leg muscles.

How can a motor image apply to spelling? Have you ever said of the spelling of a word you have in mind: "That may not be correct. Wait until I write it"? If so, you have called upon a motor image (hand-motor memory) to aid your visual memory. Motor memory is, for some people, a powerful aid in spelling; they apparently can actually feel the motions called into play by writing. You can close your eyes and without conscious thought write your signature entirely from "feel": this is motor memory.

The more mental images you have of words, the better your spelling will become. Visual, auditory, and motor images can aid in recalling correct spellings. This fundamental principle of the human mental process has an enormously important bearing on learning to spell and explains why some methods are ineffective and wasteful. For one example, you may have tried to learn the spelling of some word by repeating its letters to yourself over and over. If you have an especially well developed "auditory memory," this method may work. But auditory images are difficult or impossible for many people to summon up. In fact, some psychologists maintain it is the least developed means of recall for most of us. Mouthing words over and over is a complete waste of time for a majority of people.

When you were in school and misspelled a word, your teacher may have required you to write it correctly ten, twenty, or a hundred times. Such drill was designed to fix the word so firmly in your motor memory that you would never misspell it again. Unfortunately, such drill can, and often does, become rote; you perform the exercise without conscious attention to what you're doing. You are expending muscular effort but not relating it to visual or auditory images. We all realize that we perform certain acts with little or no conscious attention so that we are hardly aware of the process involved: shifting automobile gears, sewing, walking, carrying food to our mouths with a fork, even reading. But learning to spell requires attention and concentration, not rote methods that have little or no relationship to forming important mental images.

SIX PATHS TO CORRECT SPELLING

Learning to spell is an individual matter. What works for you may not work for your friend, and vice versa. (It's even possible, but not likely, that some people can learn to spell words by mouthing them or writing them down a hundred times.) But there are a half-dozen approaches which may be effective. One or more may work for you, depending upon your mental make-up. Almost surely, one method will be better than others for you.

My suggestion is that you select a small group of words whose spelling causes you difficulty. Try studying them in turn by the methods mentioned below and developed in succeeding chapters. It should be fairly simple to decide which approach works best for you—that is, which is quickest, surest, and has the longest lasting effects.

These six methods, discussed fully in chapters which follow, have worked for millions of people. Each is psychologically sound; each has individual merits. But not all of them will work for you. If you can't "visualize" words (the most helpful approach for the largest number of people) don't lose heart; one of the other methods may suit your individual mental processes far better. Here, then, are the six methods.

1. **Actually see words as well as hear them.**
2. **Pronounce words carefully and correctly.**
3. **Use a dictionary.**
4. **Learn a few simple rules of spelling.**
5. **Spell carefully.**
6. **Use memory devices.**

3

ACTUALLY SEE WORDS AS WELL AS HEAR THEM

As was pointed out in Chapter 2, visual memory is part of everyone's mental equipment. It is better developed in some people than in others, but each of us has at least a trace. Otherwise, we could hardly recognize a sight or a person previously noticed with only casual observation. You do not need to undertake a feature-by-feature examination to distinguish George from Sam: you know instantly, from visual memory, which friend is which. No matter how poorly developed, your visual memory is a storehouse of familiar images.

The ability to visualize words, to see them in the mind's eye, is the hallmark of the good speller. To mix some metaphors, it is his "ace in the hole," his "secret weapon." When a word is mentioned, a proficient speller can "see" the word in full detail, every letter standing out, as though it were written on paper, or the floor, the wall, the sky—against whatever background object he calls to mind. If you are a poor speller, you lack this ability to some degree. Why is this so?

Perhaps one reason is that you learned to read words as units and were not required to sound them out letter-by-letter and syllable-by-syllable. Such a method of teaching was partly a protest against the chaotic or nonexistent relationship between sound and symbol in many English words. This approach also recognized that we *do* read words as units, not as successions of letters. Possibly this "modern" method of teaching reading helped to create many poor spellers.

It is quite possible to learn the general appearance of words on flash cards and later to recognize them elsewhere. You have no difficulty in visualizing such words as *cat, hat, dog,* and *run.* But unless you have actually studied them, you may mistake *their* for *there,* or *its* for *it's,* to mention only two examples of oft-misspelled words. (Fortunately, most teachers have long since modified this new approach and now teach not only by word units but also by sounds, letters, and syllables.)

YOUR PERCEPTION SPAN

Again, your difficulty in visualizing words may have to do with your perception span. Some people can form a remarkably definite and complete impression of an entire room at a single glance; others can look at the same room for minutes on end without really "seeing" it at all. Similarly, many words contain too many letters for some people to take in at a single glance; possibly three to five letters is all they can perceive at one time. (Please remember that we are here discussing not reading but accurate and detailed mental pictures.)

If your ability to "see words in your mind" is weak and faulty, begin by dividing the words you are studying into syllables. Then you can focus on one syllable at a time (usually two to five letters) and not stretch your perception (seeing) span beyond reasonable limits. After learning to "see" each syllable separately, you can more and more easily visualize the complete word made up of separately seen units. For example, if you cannot mentally see the word *compete*, focus first on *com* and then on *pete*. When you have learned to see each unit, you can readily see them combined. If you cannot "see" the word *competitively*, try focusing on each of the individual units and then combine them: *com-pet-i-tive-ly*. (See Chapter 12.)

A principle of photography may be of help with this problem. What we call a snapshot is an instantaneous photograph—a picture taken with a small amount of exposure time. Other pictures require longer exposure for varying reasons. Simple words like *cat, dog, boy*, and *am* may be called snapshots—they make an instantaneous clear image on the mind. But words like *cataclysm, dogged, boycott*, and *amphibious* require longer exposure. That is, you must look at them, probably by syllables, long enough to form clear and precise mental images of them.

When you have a strong, completely established mental picture of a word, you can spell it on any occasion without hesitation or difficulty. The greatest single mistake of the poor speller is not looking at a word with enough care and time to fix it in his mind firmly and forever. Don't say that you can't do this; you already have done so with many words. You can picture and spell without hesitation many simple and even some very complex words. You can do this for your own name, for your town or city, and for the street on which you live. That is, you have looked at these words and have actually *seen* what you looked at.

HOW TO "SEE" WORDS MENTALLY

Here is a good method of learning to "see" words mentally:

1. With your eyes on the word being studied, pronounce it carefully. If you don't know the proper pronunciation, consult a dictionary.
2. Study each individual letter in the word; if the word has more than one syllable, separate the syllables and focus on each one in turn.
3. *Close your eyes* and pronounce and spell the word either letter-by-letter or syllable-by-syllable, depending upon its length.
4. Look at the word again to make certain that you have recalled it correctly.
5. Practice this alternate fixing of the image and its recall until you are certain that you can instantly "see" the word under any circumstances and at any time.

Such a procedure is especially valuable when dealing with tricky words which add or drop letters for no apparent reason; which contain silent letters; or which transpose or change letters without logical cause:

explain but *explanation*	*curious* but *curiosity*
proceed but *procedure*	*maintain* but *maintenance*
pronounce but *pronunciation*	*fire* but *fiery*

The most frequent error in visualizing words is mistaking one for another similar to it. A *homograph* is a word identical with another and therefore causes no spelling trouble, whatever difficulty it may provide in pronunciation and correct usage. The *bow* in *bow tie* is spelled the same as the word *bow,* meaning "to bend," but differs in pronunciation and meaning.

Homonyms, however, do cause spelling trouble. They are words identical in pronunciation but with different meanings and often with different spellings. If you spell *bore* when you mean *boar,* or *meet* when you mean *meat,* you have incurred homonym trouble.

The only sure remedy for this type of blunder is to study such words until they and their meanings are fixed in your mind.

You should understand the meanings of each of the following words and not use one when you mean another. If you will concentrate on each individual word and its meaning as suggested in the five steps on page 18, you should be able to bring it to mind whenever you have occasion to use it. The words in each group in the following list resemble each other in some way, although many of them are neither homonyms nor homographs. Carefully "seeing" them will remove your spelling problems with this class of words. Pronunciation is still another matter; not all of the grouped words which follow are pronounced identically, but all those in one group do have some resemblance to each other.

This list is far from complete. Hundreds of additional words could have been included, but those given here are the ones most often confused. Also, please remember that some of the words which follow have more than one part of speech. Usually, only one part of speech is indicated, since we are concentrating on spelling rather than grammar. Again, not all meanings are provided for every word. Consult your dictionary if you need further information about variant meanings of the words and word groups which follow.

LOOK-ALIKES AND SOUND-ALIKES

1. **Accede**—To agree or consent. I *accede* to your request.
   Exceed—To surpass. Don't *exceed* the speed limit.
2. **Accent**—Emphasis in speaking. Put more *accent* on the first syllable.
   Ascent—A rising, a going up. The path has a steep *ascent.*
   Assent—Consent, agreement. The proposal easily won our *assent.*
3. **Accept**—To receive. Joan would not *accept* the gift.
   Except—To omit or exempt. The soldier was *excepted* from guard duty that day.
4. **Access**—Admittance, way or approach. He has *access* to the vaults.
   Excess—Surpassing limits. The meeting was marked by an *excess* of good feeling.

5. **Adapt**—To change, make suitable. He *adapted* himself to the new plan.

   Adept—Skilled, expert. Joan was *adept* in cooking.

   Adopt—To choose, select. I shall *adopt* your proposal.

6. **Adverse**—Hostile, opposed. George had an *adverse* opinion.

   Averse—Unwilling, reluctant. He was *averse* to joining us.

7. **Advice**—Counsel (a noun). Please accept my *advice*.

   Advise—To give counsel (a verb). I *advise* you to go.

8. **Affect**—To influence, produce change. Your plan *affects* my purpose.

   Effect—Result, change. What will be the *effect* of your decision?

9. **Air**—Mixture of gases. He likes to breathe fresh *air*.

   Heir—One who inherits. She was my daughter and only *heir*.

10. **Aisle**—Passageway, corridor. Mary walked slowly down the *aisle*.

    Isle—Land surrounded by water. He wants to live on a deserted *isle*.

11. **Alimentary**—Connected with food, nutrition. The surgeon removed an obstruction in Sue's *alimentary* canal.

    Elementary—Connected with rudiments, fundamentals. The little boy has just started *elementary* school.

12. **Allay**—To rest, to relieve. Medicine will *allay* your pain.

    Alley—Narrow passage. This *alley* leads nowhere.

    Alleys—Narrow passages (plural). The city has many blind *alleys*.

    Allies—Partners, comrades (plural). The *Allies* defeated Germany.

    Ally—To join with (verb), one who joins (noun). Please *ally* yourself with our campaign. England has often been an *ally* of the United States.

13. **All ready**—All are ready. We'll leave when we are *all ready*.

    Already—Earlier, previously. When we arrived, Bill had *already* left.

14. **All together**—All in company. The family was *all together* for the event.

    Altogether—Wholly, completely. He was not *altogether* pleased by the outcome of the election.

15. **Allude**—To make reference to. The speaker *alluded* to the bad record of his opponents.

Elude—To escape, to evade. Big money has always *eluded* my group of friends.

16. **Allusion**—A reference to (noun). He made an *allusion* to those not present.

    Illusion—Deception (noun). This is an optical *illusion*.

17. **Altar**—Place of worship (noun). Many knelt at the *altar*.

    Alter—To change (verb). Do not *alter* your scheme.

18. **Always**—Continually, forever. I shall *always* love Joy.

    All ways—Without exception. He is prepared in *all ways* to do the job.

19. **Amateur**—Nonprofessional. He is an *amateur* chef.

    Armature—Armorlike covering. The *armature* of this dynamo needs repair.

20. **An**—One, each. This is *an* excellent report

    And—Also, plus. He ate a peach *and* a pear.

21. **Angel**—Celestial being. You are far from being an *angel*.

    Angle—Geometric figure. The *angle* of the street was sharp.

22. **Ante-** —Prefix meaning "before," "prior." She waited in the dentist's *anteroom*.

    Anti- —Prefix meaning "opposite," "against." Iodine is an effective *antiseptic*.

23. **Appraise**—To judge, to estimate. The diamond was *appraised* at one carat.

    Apprise—To inform, notify. We *apprised* him of his election.

24. **Are**—Form of the verb "to be." We *are* ready to eat.

    Or—Conjunction suggesting an alternative. Pay the price *or* walk out.

    Our—Form of the pronoun "we." This is *our* job.

25. **Assay**—A test or to test. He began to *assay* the mineral.

    Essay—An attempt or to try. He *essayed* the difficult job.

26. **Assure**—To convince, to guarantee. I *assured* him of my good will.

    Insure—To secure. He *insured* his house against fire.

27. **Attendance**—An attending, meeting. The *attendance* was greater than expected.

    Attendants—Persons present. The bride had nine *attendants*.

28. **Aught**—Any little part, any respect. For *aught* I know, you are correct.

    Ought—Indicating duty, obligation. Every citizen *ought* to vote.

Naught—Nothing, zero. Our efforts availed *naught.*

29. **Bail**—Deposited credit. The accused was free on *bail.*
Bale—Package or bundle. The stevedores hauled *bales* of cotton from the ship.

30. **Baited**—Holding bait. My fishhook was then *baited.*
Bated—Held in. We watched with *bated* breath.

31. **Ball**—Round object. Nan threw the *ball* to me.
Bole—Tree trunk. The *bole* was twenty inches in diameter.
Boll—Pod of a plant. This is a cotton *boll.*
Bowl—A receptacle (noun) or to roll (verb). This is a china *bowl.* He likes to *bowl* every night.

32. **Baring**—Uncovering. There he stood, *baring* his head to the rain.
Barring—Excepting. *Barring* the captain, everyone was in the lifeboat.
Bearing—Carrying, enduring. He is *bearing* up under grave difficulties.

33. **Bazaar**—Market, shop. The church had a *bazaar* to raise money for the altar.
Bizarre—Odd, queer. The clown's appearance was *bizarre.*

34. **Beach**—Sandy shore, strand. Atlantic City has a famous *beach.*
Beech—Tree. Peel the bark from that *beech.*

35. **Bear**—To carry (verb) or mammal (noun). People must *bear* their burdens. There is a *bear* in the zoo.
Bare—Uncovered, empty. This is a *bare* room.

36. **Beat**—To hit or to strike. He *beat* the rug to clean it.
Beet—A plant. The *beet* is a source of sugar.

37. **Berry**—Fruit. This is a small, juicy *berry.*
Bury—To preserve, conceal. Please *bury* the evidence.

38. **Berth**—Place to sleep. Henry slept in a lower *berth.*
Birth—Act of being born. His *birth* occurred in 1930.

39. **Biding**—Waiting, expecting. The nominee was *biding* his time.
Bidding—Command, summons (noun). The *bidding* for property was brisk.

40. **Blew**—Past tense of "blow." The wind *blew* hard.
Blue—Color. He wore a *blue* shirt.

41. **Bloc**—Group of people. They formed a solid *bloc* in the campaign.

Block—A solid (noun) or to impede (verb). This is a heavy *block* of stone. Don't try to *block* this action.

42. **Boar**—Male hog. He shot a splendid wild *boar*.
Bore—To drill or dig. He thinks we should *bore* for water at this place.

43. **Board**—Flat piece of wood. The *board* was heavy.
Bored—Wearied. He was *bored* by the meeting.

44. **Boarder**—Lodger. Mr. Jones is a new *boarder* at this house.
Border—Boundary or frontier. The river forms a *border* between the two states.

45. **Boer**—Dutch colonist. He is a *Boer* from South Africa.
Boor—Ill-mannered person. He acted like a *boor*.

46. **Born**—Given birth to. Mamie was *born* in 1935.
Borne—Form of "to bear." The casket was *borne* to the grave.
Bourn (bourne)—Goal or limit. "The undiscovered country from whose *bourne* no traveler returns."

47. **Borough**—Governmental unit. She lives in the *borough* of Queens.
Borrow—To receive with the intention of returning. He wants to *borrow* my coat.
Burro—Donkey. I'll ride the horse; you ride the *burro*.

48. **Brake**—Device for stopping. The *brake* on this truck needs repair.
Break—To separate, destroy. Be careful not to *break* the glasses.

49. **Bread**—Food. Give her a slice of *bread*.
Bred—Hatched, born. This is a finely *bred* horse.

50. **Breadth**—Distance, width. The box is four inches in *breadth*.
Breath—Exhalation. His *breath* froze in the cold air.
Breathe—To inhale or exhale air. Please *breathe* slowly and deeply.

51. **Brewed**—Fermented, steeped. Jane *brewed* a cup of tea.
Brood—Offspring. The hen had a large *brood* of chicks.

52. **Bridal**—Referring to a bride. You are invited to the *bridal* supper.
Bridle—Headgear for an animal. The horse objects to his new *bridle*.

53. **Britain**—Short for *Great Britain*. London is the capital of *Britain*.
Briton—An Englishman. He is proud to be a *Briton*.

54. **Broach**—To bring up (verb). Let's not *broach* that subject.

Brooch—Pin with a clasp. She wore an expensive *brooch*.

55. **Build**—To make, establish. Let's *build* our home here.

Billed—Form of "to bill." He was *billed* for the entire sum.

56. **Bullion**—Ingots. Much gold *bullion* is stored at Fort Knox.

Bouillon—Broth. The patient ate a cup of chicken *bouillon*.

57. **Calendar**—Table, register. I have no appointments on my *calendar*.

Calender—Machine with rollers. The *calender* gave the cloth a glossy finish.

Colander—Pan with perforations. Use a *colander* for washing lettuce.

58. **Calvary**—Name of a hill outside Jerusalem. Jesus was crucified on *Calvary*.

Cavalry—Troops on horseback. Stonewall Jackson was a *cavalry* leader.

59. **Cannon**—Large gun. Men pulled the *cannon* into position.

Canon—Law or rule. He lives by the *canon* of good taste.

60. **Canvas**—Cloth. The *canvas* was stiff with mud.

Canvass—To solicit, request. Please *canvass* the block for donations.

61. **Capital**—For all meanings other than "a building." He raised *capital* for the work.

Capitol—A building. Many sightseers go to the state *capitol*.

62. **Carat**—Weight. The stone weighs two *carats*.

Caret—Mark. Insert a *caret* to show the missing letter.

Carrot—Vegetable. Scrape the *carrots* slowly.

63. **Casual**—Not planned, incidental. This is a *casual* visit.

Causal—Relating to cause and effect. A *causal* factor in his decision was illness.

64. **Ceiling**—Overhanging expanse. Your room has a high *ceiling*.

Sealing—Fastening, closing. Try *sealing* the envelope more carefully.

65. **Censer**—Incense burner. There is a lovely ornamented *censer* in the church.

Censor—To examine. I do not wish you to *censor* my mail.

Censure—To condemn. The judge will strongly *censure* your action.

66. **Cent**—Coin. It's not worth a *cent*.

Scent—Odor. The *scent* of the skunk was powerful.

67. **Charted**—Mapped. The trapper *charted* the wilderness.
    Chartered—Hired, engaged. We *chartered* a bus for the picnic.
68. **Chased**—Pursued, followed. Joe often *chased* after pretty girls.
    Chaste—Pure, unsullied. A *chaste* reputation is considered priceless.
69. **Choir**—Group of singers. Joy sings in a church *choir* every week.
    Quire—Measurement of paper. He used up a *quire* of paper.
70. **Choose**—To pick out, select. I do not *choose* to go today.
    Chose—Past tense of "to choose." I *chose* not to go yesterday.
71. **Chord**—Combination of musical tones. The pianist played the opening *chords*.
    Cord—String or rope. Tie this package with a strong *cord*.
72. **Cite**—To summon, quote. Please *cite* your authority.
    Sight—View, vision. The valley was a beautiful *sight*.
    Site—Location. This is a good *site* for our camp.
73. **Claws**—Talons, curved nails. This kitten has sharp *claws*.
    Clause—Group of words. This sentence has no dependent *clause*.
74. **Climactic**—Pertaining to climax. This was the *climactic* scene in the drama.
    Climatic—Pertaining to climate. He likes the *climatic* conditions in Florida.
75. **Clothes**—Body covering. Tom bought a suit of *clothes*.
    Cloths—Pieces of cloth. Dirty dish *cloths* hung near the sink.
76. **Coarse**—Unrefined, common. The driver's *coarse* speech offended the passengers.
    Course—Way or passage. He took the easy *course*.
77. **Coma**—Unconsciousness. Mr. Jones fell into a deep *coma*.
    Comma—Mark of punctuation. This word should be followed by a *comma*.
78. **Complacent**—Smug, self-satisfied. Your attitude is annoyingly *complacent*.
    Complaisant—Obliging. The patient was *complaisant* about hospital routine.
79. **Complement**—Something that completes. This necklace will *complement* your dress.
    Compliment—Flattery. She enjoyed the *compliment* paid to her.
80. **Comprehensible**—Understandable. To be *comprehensible* use nontechnical language.

Comprehensive—Inclusive, including much. This was a *comprehensive* account of the battle.

81. **Confidant**—One trusted with secrets. Jill made David her *confidant*.

Confident—Assured, certain. Jack was *confident* of success.

82. **Conscience**—Sense of right and wrong. His *conscience* began to bother him.

Conscious—Awake, able to feel and think. The injured boy was still *conscious*.

83. **Conscientiousness**—Uprightness, honesty. The notary was rewarded for his *conscientiousness*.

Consciousness—Awareness. The victim died before regaining *consciousness*.

84. **Consul**—An official. He called the American *consul* at Naples.

Council—Assembly, group. This is a *council* of older citizens.

Counsel—Advice. The physician gave me sound *counsel*.

85. **Coral**—Skeletons of marine animals. The ship foundered on a *coral* reef.

Corral—Pen or enclosure. This ranch needs a better *corral* for horses.

86. **Core**—Center. The *core* of an apple is not edible.

Corps—Group of people. They were assigned to a *corps* of engineers.

Corpse—Dead body. The *corpse* was carried to the local cemetery.

87. **Corporal**—Concerning the body (adjective), or low-ranking officer (noun). The teacher does not approve of *corporal* punishment. He was promoted to the rank of *corporal*.

Corporeal—Material, tangible. He left no *corporeal* property.

88. **Costume**—Clothing. Your *costume* is too colorful.

Custom—Established practice. It was his *custom* to walk there every day.

89. **Creak**—To make a sound. He felt as though his very bones would *creak*.

Creek—Small stream. Bill waded in the *creek*.

90. **Crews**—Seamen or groups of persons. The *crews* of all vessels were discharged.

Cruise—Voyage. They left on a *cruise* around the world.

91. **Currant**—Small, seedless raisin. This recipe for fruit cake requires the use of *currants*.
   Current—A stream (noun) or contemporary (adjective). This river has a swift *current*. I like to read about *current* events.
92. **Cymbal**—Musical instrument. Is the *cymbal* made of brass or bronze?
   Symbol—Sign or token. The flag is a *symbol* of our country.
93. **Dairy**—Milk enterprise. He drove the cows from the field to the *dairy*.
   Diary—Daily record. Eleanor kept a *diary* during her entire trip.
94. **Days**—Plural of "day." I was in the hospital for ten *days*.
   Daze—To dazzle or stupefy. The policeman was *dazed* by a sharp blow.
95. **Dear**—Beloved, precious, expensive. Bill is my *dear* friend.
   Deer—Animal. Usually only the male *deer* has antlers.
96. **Decease**—Death. He was buried two days after his *decease*.
   Disease—Sickness. This *disease* must run its course.
97. **Decent**—Respectable, suitable. Please wear a *decent* hat.
   Descent—Act of descending. The *descent* from the mountain top was slow.
   Dissent—To differ, disagree. I *dissent* from your opinion.
98. **Definite**—Explicit, clear. The speaker made a *definite* proposal.
   Definitive—Decisive, final, complete. This is the *definitive* biography of Mrs. Siddons.
99. **Dependence**—Condition of being supported. My *dependence* upon you is complete.
   Dependents—Those supported by others. He claimed six *dependents* on his tax return.
100. **Deprecate**—To express disapproval. He *deprecated* his own efforts.
   Depreciate—To lower in value. The property *depreciated* quickly.
101. **Des′ert**—Barren ground. The *desert* is two hundred miles wide.
   De sert′—To leave behind. Don't *desert* your friends.
   Dessert—Sweet food. Ice cream is my favorite *dessert*.
102. **Detract**—To lower the quality of, to reduce the value of. His loud voice *detracted* from his personality.

Distract—To divert. Don't *distract* me with radio music.

103. **Device**—Contrivance (noun). The inventor came up with a clever *device*.

Devise—To make, invent (verb). The coach will *devise* a plan for winning the game.

104. **Die**—To cease to live. Everyone must *die* sometime.

Dye—To color. I wish to *dye* this dress.

105. **Dining**—Eating. This is a pretty *dining* room.

Dinning—Pertaining to noise, uproar. The sound of the wheels was *dinning* in my ears.

106. **Discomfit**—To frustrate, thwart. Your proposal will *discomfit* my hopes and plans.

Discomfort—Uneasiness, distress. His broken leg caused him *discomfort*.

107. **Discreet**—Judicious, thoughtful. You should be more *discreet* when talking to the boss.

Discrete—Separate, distinct. These two problems are *discrete*.

108. **Divers**—Several or sundry. She has *divers* means of support.

Diverse—Different, varied. Their personalities were powerful but *diverse*.

109. **Dual**—Twofold. The actress has a *dual* role in this play.

Duel—Combat. Hamilton and Burr fought a *duel*.

110. **Due**—Payable. The money is *due* today.

Do—To perform, act. Kindly *do* as your foreman suggests.

111. **Emigrate**—To leave a country. The foreman *emigrated* from Poland.

Immigrate—To enter a country. Many people have tried to *immigrate* to this country.

112. **Eminent**—Noteworthy, outstanding. Mr. Hughes is an *eminent* lawyer.

Imminent—Near at hand. Outbreak of war is *imminent*.

113. **Envel′ op**—To cover, wrap up. Fire caused smoke to *envelop* the block.

En′ velope—A covering. This *envelope* has no postage stamp.

114. **Errand**—Trip or task. Please run this *errand* for me.

Errant—Roving, wandering, mistaken. Please correct your *errant* behavior.

Arrant—Notorious. The soldier proved himself an *arrant* coward.

115. **Ever**—Always. He is *ever* in a jovial mood.
     Every—Without exception. *Every* person present will please stand.
116. **Exalt**—To raise, praise. Shall we *exalt* God the Father?
     Exult—To rejoice. Don't *exult* over your victory.
117. **Exceptionable**—Objectionable. Your constant tardiness is *exceptionable*.
     Exceptional—Out of the ordinary. Joy's singing is *exceptional*.
118. **Extant**—Still existing. He is the greatest musician *extant*.
     Extent—Size, length. What is the *extent* of your farm?
     Extinct—No longer existing. The dinosaur is an *extinct* beast.
119. **Factitious**—Artificial. The greatest *factitious* need of today is money.
     Fictitious—Imaginary. His account of the journey was entirely *fictitious*.
120. **Fain**—Ready, eager (rarely used). She would *fain* go with you.
     Feign—To invent, fabricate. The sailor *feigned* illness.
121. **Faint**—To lose consciousness. I feel as if I am about to *faint*.
     Feint—To pretend, deceive. The player *feinted* his opponent out of position.
122. **Fair**—All uses except those for "fare." The day was cold and *fair*.
     Fare—To travel (verb); transportation money (noun). I shall soon *fare* forth. Please pay your *fare*.
123. **Find**—To discover. Try to *find* happiness where you can.
     Fined—Punished. The motorist was *fined* fifty dollars.
124. **Fir**—Tree. This is a grove of beautiful *firs*.
     Fur—Animal hair. This coat has a collar of *fur*.
125. **Flair**—Talent, ability. She has a certain *flair* for designing clothes.
     Flare—To blaze up. The fire suddenly *flared* up.
126. **Flea**—Insect. The *flea* is a small, wingless creature.
     Flee—To run away. We had to *flee* from the burning house.
127. **Flour**—Ground grain. This is enough *flour* to feed us.
     Flower—A blossom. The rose is Gray's favorite *flower*.
128. **Flout**—To mock, to scoff. She was determined to *flout* all convention.
     Flaunt—To make a gaudy display. He *flaunted* his new prosperity all over the city.

129. **Fondling**—Caressing, coddling. Will you stop *fondling* that cat?
     Foundling—Abandoned child. This is a home for *foundlings*.
130. **Forbear**—To refrain: I cannot *forbear* telling you this.
     Forebear—Ancestor. His *forebears* came from Greece.
131. **Foreword**—Preface, introduction. This book needs no *foreword*.
     Forward—Movement onward. The troops marched *forward*.
132. **Formally**—Ceremoniously. The envoy greeted us *formally*.
     Formerly—Earlier. He was *formerly* a champion.
133. **Fort**—Enclosed place, fortified building. The attackers burned the *fort*.
     Forte—Special accomplishment. His *forte* is outdoor cooking.
134. **Forth**—Onward. I shall be with you from this day *forth*.
     Fourth—Next after third. The *Fourth* of July is a holiday.
135. **Freeze**—To congeal with cold. He asked me to *freeze* the vegetables.
     Frieze—Architectural term. The castle had several beautiful *friezes* on the walls.
136. **Funeral**—Ceremonies at burial. The *funeral* was attended by hundreds of friends.
     Funereal—Sad, dismal. Molly wore a *funereal* look.
137. **Gait**—Manner of moving. This saddle horse has four excellent *gaits*.
     Gate—Door or opening. Open the *gate* and come in.
138. **Gamble**—To wager, bet. He *gambled* on cards and dice.
     Gambol—To skip about. The children *gamboled* on the village green.
139. **Genius**—Great ability. Beethoven was a man of *genius*.
     Genus—Class, kind. What is the *genus* of this plant?
140. **Gibe**—To scorn or sneer at. I'm trying hard; don't *gibe* at me.
     Jibe—Same meaning as "gibe" but also "to change direction." The boat *jibed* twice on the homeward run.
141. **Gild**—To overlay with gold. Please *gild* this vase.
     Guild—Association, union. Sam belonged to a *guild* of craftsmen.
142. **Gilt**—Gold on surface. This glass has a layer of *gilt*.
     Guilt—Wrongdoing, crime. He immediately announced his *guilt*.
143. **Gorilla**—Manlike ape. This *gorilla* is five feet tall.
     Guerrilla—Irregular soldier. He belonged to a band of *guerrillas*.

144. **Gourmand**—Large eater. Diamond Jim Brady was a *gourmand.*
Gourmet—Fastidious eater, epicure. Many French people are notable *gourmets.*

145. **Grip**—Act of holding firmly. He took a firm *grip* on the tire.
Gripe—To pinch, to distress. What he ate had *griped* his digestive system.

146. **Grisly**—Horrible, ghastly. The execution was a *grisly* scene.
Gristly—Pertaining to tough, elastic tissue. This is a *gristly* cut of meat.
Grizzly—Grizzled, gray; pertaining to the animal. There is only one *grizzly* bear in the zoo.

147. **Hail**—To greet. We *hailed* him as our leader.
Hale—Healthy, vigorous. He wanted to be *hale* in mind and body.

148. **Hair**—Threadlike outgrowth. He had no *hair* on his head.
Hare—Rabbit. The dog chased the *hare* for an hour.

149. **Hart**—Male deer. The old *hart* was king of the forest.
Heart—Muscular organ. His *heart* was beating quickly.

150. **Heal**—To make sound, well. My hope is to *heal* you in mind and body.
Heel—Part of the foot. His *heel* was punctured by a nail.

151. **Hear**—To become aware of sounds. I can't *hear* you.
Here—In this place. Will you be *here* with me?

152. **Hoard**—Laid-up store. Here is where he had his *hoard* of money.
Horde—Crowd. A *horde* of riders clattered toward us.

153. **Hole**—Cavity. The boys dug a *hole* in the ground.
Whole—Intact, complete. I've told you the *whole* story.

154. **Holy**—Sacred, consecrated. A church is a *holy* place.
Wholly—Completely, entirely. I'm *wholly* on your side.

155. **Hoping**—Wanting, desiring. I'm *hoping* you will accept my invitation.
Hopping—Leaping, springing. I'm *hopping* a train tonight.

156. **Human**—A person. He was a real *human,* not a mere animal.
Humane—Tender, merciful, considerate. He was a *humane* ruler of his people.

157. **Idle**—Worthless, useless, pointless. We engaged in *idle* talk.
Idol—Image. Ben made an *idol* of prestige.

158. **Immunity**—Exemption from duty. Heart disease gave him *immunity* from military service.

Impunity—Exemption from punishment. He could eat with *impunity* whatever he pleased.

159. **Impassable**—Not passable. The road over the mountain was *impassable*.
Impossible—Incapable of being accomplished. The order was *impossible* to carry out.

160. **Incidence**—Range of occurrence, influence. The *incidence* of influenza was high that winter.
Incidents—Events, happenings. Which *incidents* of your trip did you enjoy the most?

161. **Indict**—To accuse, charge with crime. He was *indicted* for theft.
Indite—To write, compose. He *indited* a beautiful letter to the sorrowing widow.

162. **Ingenious**—Clever, tricky. This is an *ingenious* computer.
Ingenuous—Innocent, artless. She is an *ingenuous* young girl.

163. **Invade**—To enter, intrude. The soldiers were soon ordered to *invade* our country.
Inveighed—Attacked in words, assailed. He *inveighed* against all his enemies.

164. **Its**—Possessive pronoun. This company should have *its* proper place in history.
It's—"It is." *It's* a delightful day.

165. **Jealous**—Resentful, envious. Mary is *jealous* of Jane's beauty.
Zealous—Diligent, devoted. The senator was *zealous* in committee work.

166. **Knave**—Unprincipled man or boy. The attorney called the gangster a *knave*.
Nave—Part of a church. Chairs were placed in the *nave*.

167. **Knew**—To have fixed in mind or memory. The salesman *knew* all the buyer's objections.
New—Of recent origin. This is a *new* model.

168. **Know**—To understand, perceive. Do you *know* how far it is to town?
No—Word used to express denial, dissent. *No,* I shall not go with you.

169. **Later**—Referring to time. It's *later* than you think.
Latter—Second of two. I prefer the *latter* course of action.

170. **Lead**—Conduct, guide. John will *lead* the choral group.
Lead—A metal. This is a *lead* pipe.

Led—Past tense of "to lead." Grant *led* his soldiers into Vicksburg.

171. **Leaf**—Outgrowth of a stem. This is a lovely oak *leaf.*
Lief—Gladly, willingly. I'd as *lief* go as stay.

172. **Lean**—Scant of fat, flesh. This is a *lean* strip of bacon.
Lien—Legal right. He procured a *lien* on the property.

173. **Least**—Smallest, slightest. This was the *least* of my worries.
Lest—For fear that. Please keep writing *lest* we forget you.

174. **Lessen**—To become less, diminish. Now all your financial problems will *lessen.*
Lesson—Something to be learned. May this be a *lesson* to you.

175. **Levee**—Embankment. The river overflowed the *levee.*
Levy—To impose. The judge will *levy* a large fine.

176. **Lie**—Falsehood. He told me a *lie.*
Lye—Alkaline substance. Keep this bottle of *lye* away from children.

177. **Lifelong**—For all one's life. His *lifelong* desire was to go to Europe.
Livelong—Whole, entire. Birds sing the *livelong* day.

178. **Lightening**—Making less heavy. His kindness was *lightening* my weight of sorrow.
Lightning—Discharge of electricity. The rain was preceded by thunder and *lightning.*

179. **Lineament**—Feature, characteristic. What is the most noticeable *lineament* of his face?
Liniment—Medicated liquid. The trainer rubbed the boxer's legs with *liniment.*

180. **Liqueur**—Highly flavored alcoholic drink. Joe's favorite after-dinner *liqueur* was chartreuse.
Liquor—Distilled or spirituous beverage. Scotch was Abe's favorite *liquor.*

181. **Loan**—Act of granting, lending. I secured a *loan* of fifty dollars.
Lone—Solitary, standing apart. He was the *lone* rebel in the office.

182. **Loose**—Not fastened tightly. A *loose* wire caused all the trouble.
Lose—To suffer the loss of. Don't *lose* what you have gained.
Loss—A defeat. He felt keenly the *loss* of the money.

183. **Mail**—Letters, etc. The *mail* came at ten o'clock.
Male—Masculine. This cat is *male.*

184. **Main**—Chief, principal. Is this the *main* highway?
Mane—Long hair. The horse's *mane* was filled with cockleburs.
185. **Manner**—Way of doing. They treated us in a civilized *manner*.
Manor—Landed estate. Sir Charles is lord of the *manor*.
186. **Mantel**—Shelf. The *mantel* above the fireplace is of sturdy oak.
Mantle—Loose covering. Has the *mantle* of Moses descended upon this judge?
187. **Marshal**—Officer. The *marshal* arrested him.
Martial—Warlike. The governor placed the community under *martial* law.
188. **Material**—Crude or raw matter, substance. What is the *material* in your dress?
Matériel—Equipment in general. This military campaign required vast *matériel*.
189. **Maybe**—Perhaps. *Maybe* she doesn't like you.
May be—Verb form expressing possibility. It *may be* going to rain this afternoon.
190. **Meat**—Flesh. His favorite foods are *meat* and potatoes.
Meet—To come into contact. We plan to *meet* tomorrow.
191. **Medal**—Commemorative design. The major gave him a *medal* for bravery.
Meddle—To interfere. Please don't *meddle* in my business.
Metal—A hard substance obtained from ores. Gold, silver, and copper are *metals*.
Mettle—Disposition, temper. The battle revealed the soldier's *mettle*.
192. **Miner**—One who extracts minerals. He is a *miner* from Pennsylvania.
Minor—Person under legal age. A *minor* has no voting privileges.
193. **Moat**—Trench. The *moat* around the castle was filled with water.
Mote—Particle, speck. He had a *mote* of dust in each eye.
194. **Moors**—Mohammedans. Many *Moors* live in North Africa.
Moors—Open land. These flowers came from the Scottish *moors*.
Mores—Folkways, customs. *Mores* here differ from those in my country.
195. **Moral**—Good or proper. His *moral* code was high.
Morale—Condition of the spirit, state of being. The *morale* of the workers was excellent.

196. **Morning**—Early part of the day. We shall leave early tomorrow *morning*.
 Mourning—Sorrowing, grieving. The *mourning* family went to the cemetery.

197. **Motif**—Theme or subject. What is the *motif* of that composition?
 Motive—Spur or incentive. The *motive* of the murder was revenge.

198. **Naval**—Pertaining to ships. England is a great *naval* power.
 Navel—Pit or depression on the abdomen. He suffered a wound near his *navel*.

199. **Of**—Preposition with many meanings. He is a native *of* Ohio.
 Off—Away from. The car rolled *off* the highway.

200. **On**—Preposition with many meanings. Please put the bread *on* the table.
 One—Single unit or thing. He bought *one* orange for five cents.

201. **Oracle** Place or medium for consulting gods. The senator visited the Delphic *oracle*.
 Auricle—Anatomical term. The *auricle* of her left ear was infected.

202. **Oral**—Spoken. The message was *oral*, not written.
 Aural—Pertaining to the sense of hearing. After the accident, his *aural* sense was below normal.

203. **Ordinance**—Rule, decree. There is a city *ordinance* against double parking.
 Ordnance—Military weapons. Captain Baker is an instructor of *ordnance* at West Point.

204. **Oscillate**—To swing, vibrate. The pendulum of the clock *oscillates* smoothly.
 Osculate—To kiss. Some explorers say Eskimos do not *osculate*.

205. **Pail**—Bucket or other container. Please fetch a *pail* of water.
 Pale—Of whitish appearance. My face turned *pale* in fear.

206. **Pain**—Suffering, distress. John had a *pain* in his back.
 Pane—Plate of glass. The baseball shattered the *pane*.

207. **Pair**—Two of a kind. This is a new *pair* of gloves.
 Pare—To peel. He *pared* a basket of apples.

208. **Palate**—Roof of the mouth. Peanut butter sticks to my *palate*.
 Palette—Board for painters. The artist mixed an array of autumn colors on his *palette*.

Pallet—Small, makeshift bed. I was stiff and sore from a night spent on that *pallet*.

209. **Passed**—Moved by. The car *passed* us at a high speed.
     Past—Just gone by. The *past* year was a good one for me.
210. **Peace**—Freedom from disturbance. What this world needs is *peace*.
     Piece—Portion. Please give me a *piece* of pie.
211. **Pedal**—Lever. One *pedal* of the organ needed repair.
     Peddle—To hawk, sell at retail. He *peddled* fresh fruits in a residential section.
212. **Pendant**—An ornament. She wore a gold *pendant* around her neck.
     Pendent—Hanging or suspended. The *pendent* tapesty was Oriental.
213. **Persecute**—To oppress, harass. The Pilgrims were *persecuted* because of their religious beliefs.
     Prosecute—To bring legal proceedings. The district attorney *prosecuted* the case against me.
214. **Personal**—Private. This is your *personal* property.
     Personnel—Body of persons. This company has recruited interesting *personnel*.
215. **Petition**—A request. The manager read our *petition* for a coffee break.
     Partition—Division, separation. Only a thin *partition* separated the two rooms.
216. **Physic**—Medicine. The physician recommended a strong *physic*.
     Physique—Body structure. He has a robust *physique*.
     Psychic—Pertaining to the mind or soul. The gypsy claimed *psychic* powers.
217. **Pillar**—Upright shaft. The ceiling was supported by eight *pillars*.
     Pillow—Support for the head. He sleeps without a *pillow*.
218. **Pistil**—Seed-bearing organ. This is the *pistil* of a flowering plant.
     Pistol—Small firearm. The sheriff carried his *pistol* in a holster.
219. **Plain**—Simple, or a level stretch of ground. He prefers *plain* foods. This *plain* contains hundreds of acres.
     Plane—Carpenters' tool, or level of existence. Try smoothing it with a *plane*. Your families are on the same financial *plane*.
220. **Portion**—Part, quantity. This is a larger *portion* of the roast.
     Potion—A drink. He drank the fiery *potion*.

221. **Pray**—To beseech, entreat. Please *pray* for my safety.
     Prey—Plunder, booty. The eagle is a bird of *prey*.
222. **Precede**—To come or go before. Will you *precede* me into the room?
     Proceed—To advance. He then *proceeded* to the next town.
223. **Prescribe**—To direct, order. The physician will *prescribe* a cure.
     Proscribe—To banish, to outlaw. Caesar ordered that he be *proscribed*.
224. **Principal**—Chief, foremost. He had a *principal* part in the action.
     Principle—Rule or truth. This is a sound *principle* to follow.
225. **Prophecy**—Prediction (noun). What is your *prophecy* about the future?
     Prophesy—To foretell (verb). He could *prophesy* the results.
226. **Propose**—To put forth a plan. I *propose* that we take a vote.
     Purpose—Intention, aim. What is your *purpose?*
227. **Quarts**—Measure. This bucket will hold eight *quarts*.
     Quartz—Mineral. The geologist discovered *quartz* deposits near here.
228. **Quay**—Wharf. The ship was anchored a hundred yards from the *quay*.
     Key—Instrument for locking, unlocking. Sue lost the *key* to her apartment.
229. **Quiet**—Still, calm. It was a *quiet* meeting.
     Quit—To stop, desist. He *quit* his job on Friday.
     Quite—Positive, entirely. I have not *quite* finished the book.
230. **Rabbit**—A rodent of the hare family. Mrs. MacGregor put him into a *rabbit* stew.
     Rabid—Extreme, intense, or mad with rabies. He was known as a *rabid* partisan.
     Rarebit—Welsh rabbit. The pronunciation should be "Welsh rabbit," not "Welsh *rarebit*."
231. **Rain**—Precipitation. We had four inches of *rain* last week.
     Reign—Rule. Queen Elizabeth I had a long *reign*.
     Rein—Check, curb. Lena could not *rein* in her mare going for the barn.
232. **Raise**—To lift, elevate. Please *raise* your eyes and look at me.
     Raze—To tear down. The wreckers will *raze* the building.
     Rise—To get up. When the president enters, everyone should *rise*.

233. **Rebound**—To spring back. His spirits *rebounded* at the good news.
  Redound—To have a result or effect. Your excellent performance will *redound* to your credit.

234. **Reck**—To have care or concern. He *recks* not the costs involved.
  Wreck—Destruction, damage. Hard living made him a *wreck* of a man.

235. **Reek**—Vapor, fume. There is a *reek* of turpentine in this room.
  Wreak—To give vent to. He *wreaked* his anger on the secretarial pool.

236. **Respectably**—Properly, decently. The widow lived quietly and *respectably*.
  Respectfully—With esteem, honor. He closed the letter "*Respectfully* yours."
  Respectively—In order. He referred to Tom, Dick, and Harry *respectively*.

237. **Retch**—To try to vomit. He *retched* several times and then lay still.
  Wretch—Miserable person. The poor *wretch* had threadbare clothing.

238. **Reverend**—Title for clergymen. The *Reverend* Stanley Smith is our pastor.
  Reverent—Characterized by respect, sacredness. The audience was in a *reverent* mood.

239. **Right**—Correct, or direction. What is the *right* way to town? Turn *right*, not left.
  Rite—Ceremony. The *rite* of burial was indeed solemn.

240. **Sail**—Material to catch wind. The *sails* were fluttering in the breeze.
  Sale—Special offering of goods. He bought a suit which was on *sale*.

241. **Satire**—Work that expresses ridicule or contempt. He wrote a *satire* on office parties.
  Satyr—Woodland deity, a lecherous man. John is more wolf than *satyr*.

242. **Scarce**—Not plentiful. The berries were *scarce* this year.
  Scare—To startle, frighten. He was *scared* by news of the epidemic.

243. **Serf**—A slave. The manager treats me as though I were his *serf*.

Surf—Waves. The boat capsized in the heavy *surf*.

244. **Serge**—Fabric. This *serge* suit cost fifty dollars.
 Surge—To swell, to increase suddenly. His anger *surged* at the insult.

245. **Shear**—To cut, clip. It is time to *shear* the sheep.
 Sheer—Very thin. Her stockings were black and very *sheer*.

246. **Shone**—Glowed. Her face *shone* with happiness.
 Shown—Appeared, made known. The salesmen have *shown* themselves to be capable.

247. **Shudder**—To shake or tremble. Reading about an accident makes me *shudder*.
 Shutter—Screen or cover. The owner painted the *shutters* green.

248. **Sleight**—Deftness. He performed several *sleight* of hand tricks.
 Slight—Slender, light. Jill is a very *slight* girl.

249. **Sole**—Single, one and only. Bernard was the *sole* survivor of the wreck.
 Soul—Spiritual entity. The minister prayed for the dying man's *soul*.

250. **Stair**—A step. Mount the *stairs* carefully.
 Stare—To gaze, glare. He stood there and *stared* at me.

251. **Stake**—Post, pole. Joan of Arc was burned at the *stake*.
 Steak—Slice of meat. We served a four-pound *steak*.

252. **Stationary**—Fixed in position. This statue is obviously *stationary*.
 Stationery—Paper for writing. I ordered a new box of *stationery*.

253. **Statue**—Sculptured likeness. His *statue* is in the museum.
 Stature—Height. He was six feet in *stature*.
 Statute—Law. This *statute* forbids gambling within city limits.

254. **Steal**—To take without permission. It is a sin to *steal* another's property.
 Steel—Metal. The sword was made of *steel*.

255. **Stile**—A step. Use the *stile;* don't vault the fence.
 Style—Manner of expression. This is furniture in the modern *style*.

256. **Stimulant**—Anything that stimulates. This drug is a heart *stimulant*.
 Stimulus—Something that rouses. His family's needs provided him with a *stimulus* to work hard.

257. **Straight**—Uncurved. The road ran *straight* for five miles.

Strait—Narrow passageway. We crossed the *Strait* of Magellan.

258. **Suit**—Clothing. This is an expensive new *suit*.

Suite—Set of rooms, or furniture. They engaged a *suite* of rooms at the hotel.

259. **Tail**—Rear appendage. This is the *tail* of a donkey.

Tale—Story. He told us a *tale* of his trip to the planetarium.

260. **Taught**—Trained, instructed. We were *taught* how to add and subtract.

Taut—Tightly stretched, tense. She gave us a *taut* smile.

261. **Than**—Particle denoting comparison. I am taller *than* Alfred.

Then—At that time. It was *then* that he left.

262. **Their**—Possessive pronoun. *Their* faces all look alike to me.

There—In or at that place. He was *there* on time.

They're—Shortened form of "they are." *They're* improving all the time.

263. **Therefor**—For this, for that. He selected a car and paid cash *therefor*.

Therefore—Consequently, hence. I have no money and *therefore* can't go.

264. **Thorough**—Complete. His examination was *thorough*.

Though—Notwithstanding, although. *Though* you may be right, I can't agree with you.

Threw—Tossed or hurled. They *threw* more wood on the fire.

Through—From one end or side to the other. Let's walk *through* this field.

265. **Timber**—Building material. He bought *timber* for a new dog-house.

Timbre—Quality of sound. I like the *timbre* of his voice.

266. **To**—Preposition with many meanings. Let's walk *to* town.

Too—More than enough, in addition. You have already said *too* much.

Two—Number after "one." There are *two* sides to this problem.

267. **Tortuous**—Winding, crooked. The path up the mountain is *tortuous*.

Torturous—Full of, or causing, torture or pain. The surgeon began a *torturous* examination of my spine.

268. **Treaties**—Agreements. Soviet Russia does not honor its *treaties*.

Treatise—Systematic discussion. The professor wrote a *treatise* on this subject.

269. **Troop**—An assembled company. The *troop* of Girl Scouts made camp.

    Troupe—Traveling actors. He joined a *troupe* of Shakespearian actors.

270. **Urban**—Characteristic of a city. Do you prefer *urban* to rural life?

    Urbane—Suave, smooth. His manner and speech were *urbane*.

271. **Vain**—Worthless, empty. He made a *vain* attempt to save money.

    Vane—Direction pointer. This is a new weather *vane*.

    Vein—Blood vessel. The knife severed a *vein*, not an artery.

272. **Venal**—Corruptible, mercenary. The *venal* judge was soon removed from office.

    Venial—Excusable, pardonable. That was a *venial* sin, not a mortal one.

273. **Vial**—Small vessel. This is a *vial* of perfume.

    Vile—Repulsive, offensive. His language was *vile*.

    Viol—Musical instrument. The *viol* was often played in the sixteenth century.

274. **Vice**—Evil practice. The reformers are opposed to *vice* in every form.

    Vise—Device for holding. The carpenter has many uses for a *vise*.

275. **Waist**—Middle section of a body. His *waist* is thirty-four inches.

    Waste—To squander, to employ uselessly. Save your energy; don't *waste* it.

276. **Waive**—To relinquish, give up. Don't *waive* your right to a jury trial.

    Wave—Ridge or swell of water. The *wave* tossed the small craft up.

277. **Want**—To wish or desire. I *want* to stay at home.

    Wont—Accustomed, used. He was *wont* to take a nap every afternoon.

    Won't—Contraction of "will not." I *won't* do what you ask.

278. **Weak**—Not strong. Your excuse is *weak*.

    Week—Period of seven days. This has been an active *week* for me.

279. **Weather**—State of atmosphere. We had good *weather* for the trip.

Whether—Conjunction implying alternatives. We didn't know *whether* to stay or go.

280. **Were**—Form of verb "to be." *Were* you there yesterday?
We're—Contraction of "we are." *We're* going with you.
Where—In or at what place. *Where* did you put it?

281. **While**—During the time that. I was working *while* you ate.
Wile—Trick, stratagem. She practiced her feminine *wiles* on my roommate.

282. **Whose**—Possessive case of "who." *Whose* pencil is that?
Who's—Contraction of "who is." *Who's* going out for coffee today?

283. **Wrench**—To twist, pull, jerk. He *wrenched* his knee when he fell.
Rinse—To wash. He *rinsed* the clothes several times.

284. **Wring**—To squeeze, press. *Wring* out your bathing suit.
Ring—Band of metal. He paid little money for the wedding *ring*.

285. **Wry**—Twisted, distorted. He made a *wry* face.
Rye—Cereal grass. This is *rye* flour.

286. **Yeller**—One who shrieks or screams. He is the *yeller* on this team.
Yellow—A color. You are wearing a beautiful *yellow* dress.

287. **Yolk**—Part of an egg. The recipe calls for six *yolks*.
Yoke—Frame or bar. The oxen were harnessed with *yokes*.

288. **Yore**—Time long past. Knights were bold in days of *yore*.
Your—Belonging to or done by you. Is this *your* idea?
You're—Contraction of "you are." *You're* going to make more money soon.

289. **Yowl**—Howl, wail. The dog's *yowl* woke him up.
Yawl—Sailboat. We sailed the *yawl* across the bay.

290. **Yule**—Christmas. This is a wonderful *yule* log.
You'll—Contraction of "you will" or "you shall." If *you'll* help me, I shall try.

4

PRONOUNCE WORDS CAREFULLY AND CORRECTLY

Just compare heart, beard, and heard,
Dies and diet, lord and word,
Sword and sward, retain and Britain,
(Mind the latter, how it's written)
Made has not the sound of bade;
Say, said, pay, paid, laid, but plaid.

—G. N. TRENITÉ
Drop Your Foreign Accent

These lines of doggerel amusingly demonstrate that pronunciation is not a safe guide to spelling. A system which tolerates, for example, *cough* and *through* is quite imperfect. (A frequently cited illustration is that if you use the sound of *f* as the *gh* in *enough,* of *i* as the *o* in *women,* and of *sh* as the *ti* of *fiction,* you can spell *fish* as *ghoti.*) For another example of confusion confounded, consider the sound of *ain,* the sound we have in *pain.* It can be, and is, represented by these entirely different spellings: compl*ain,* p*ane,* r*eign,* v*ein,* camp*aign,* champ*agne.* In fact, pronunciation is so unreliable a guide to spelling that you can quite logically spell *coffee* as *kauphy,* with not a single corresponding letter in the two words.

Every modern American dictionary presents its own system of recording pronunciation. Your first move should be to find out about that system. Read the essay on pronunciation included in the front matter (first pages) of your dictionary; every reliable dictionary contains such an article. Study the full pronunciation key provided on the inside of the front or back cover of your book, or in both places. Examine the pronunciation key appearing at the bottom of each page, or every other page, of your dictionary. Only after you have taken these steps are you in a position really to use your dictionary as a guide to pronunciation.

Pronunciation, as you already know and as your dictionary will again tell you, depends upon the *sound* given to alphabetical letters or letter combinations and upon the *accent* of emphasized syllables.

DICTIONARY SOUND SYSTEMS

Dictionary-makers have had to make up systems for representing sounds because only twenty-six letters exist to represent some 250 common spellings of sounds. The best-known set of symbols for the sounds of language is the International Phonetic Alphabet (IPA). This alphabet, applicable to many languages, including English, is accurate, but the ordinary speaker will find it hard to follow.

Your most sensible approach is to study the "pronunciation word" that appears in parentheses immediately after an entry word. It is a respelling of the word, giving the sounds of vowels and consonants by syllables, according to the pronunciation key that your dictionary has adopted. (Every dictionary compiler has chosen anywhere from forty to sixty symbols that he thinks adequate to explain problems in pronunciation.) Study the key in your dictionary to find out the various sounds of letters and letter combinations as indicated in sample words.

As an indication of the kinds of information provided about pronunciation in your dictionary, see how it represents the varied sounds of, say, the letter *o.* You will find that the sounds of *o* are indicated by some or all of these symbols:

o—as in *odd, hot, lot, ox*
ō—as in *go, open, over, no*
ô—as in *order, horn, ought*
ŏŏ—as in *took, book, look*
ōō—as in *pool, ooze, boot, too*

Each of the signs (symbols appearing with words in a pronunciation key) is a kind of diacritical mark. (The word *diacritical* comes from a Greek term meaning "capable of distinguishing," "distinctive.") Still other signs, or points, are occasionally added to letters to indicate a particular sound value. Among these are the *circumflex* (raison d'être), the *tilde* (cañon), the *umlaut* (schön), and the *cedilla* (façade). Some dictionaries supply these and other diacritical marks with individual words; other dictionaries provide a separate "foreign sounds" key. All diacritical marks are inexact in suggesting the reproduction of sounds, but their use is one further example of the pains dictionary makers have taken in trying to provide a faithful record of the sounds of language.

The matter of stress, or accent, is less involved than the pronunciation of sounds. But it is important. Examine the method your dictionary employs for indicating where accents fall in given entries. Some dictionaries provide both accent marks and syllabication periods (dots) in the entry word. Others use only dots to indicate syllabication in the entry word and insert accent marks in the "pronunciation word." Learn the methods your dictionary has provided for indicating heavy (primary) stress and less heavy (secondary) stress. Whatever devices your dictionary uses are made fully clear in an article at the front of the book.

Although standard pronunciation will not always enable you to spell correctly, the relationship between sound and spelling is only occasionally illogical.

First, not all sounds and spellings differ so much as those just cited. The examples given are designedly extreme. Actually, some relationship often exists between sound and spelling; a large number of words are spelled exactly as they sound, and many others have sounds and spellings almost alike. The words *bat, red,* and *top* are spelled as they sound to most people. Many longer words are also spelled as they sound, especially if you break them into syllables: *lone-li-ness, mem-o-ry, part-ner,* for example. The situation is not without hope.

Second, many of the words which differ most greatly in sound and spelling are those which you rarely need to use. Like almost everyone else, including good spellers, you would look up such words in a dictionary before attempting to write them; they do not have to be learned. Few people can spell, on demand, such a word as *phthisic.* They consult a dictionary, and so should you.

Third, actually *mispronouncing* words causes more trouble than does a difference between the spelling and sound of a correctly pronounced word. In other words, correct pronunciation is sometimes of little help in spelling, but *mispronouncing* often adds an additional hazard. You have noticed that this fact applies to some words in the list of "Look-Alikes and Sound-Alikes" beginning on page 19. It is probably improper pronunciation which would make you spell *Cal-*

vary when you mean *cavalry*. *Affect* and *effect* look somewhat alike, but they do have different pronunciations as well as different meanings. A *dairy* is one thing; a *diary* is another and will be so indicated by correct pronunciation. There is some reason why, from sound, you might spell *crowd* as "croud" or *benign* as "benine." But there is no reason except poor pronunciation for spelling *shudder* as "shutter," *propose* as "porpose," or *marrying* as "marring."

Spelling consciousness, an *awareness* of words, depends in part on correct pronunciation. Properly pronouncing the following words will help some people to spell them correctly. Mispronouncing them will cause nearly everyone spelling trouble. Look at each word, as suggested on page 18, until you are fully aware of it. Pronounce each word correctly, consulting your dictionary often and carefully.

The list is merely suggestive; people mispronounce so many words in so many different ways that no list can be complete. But the author has encountered faulty spellings of the words listed here and suspects that they represent fairly general mispronunciations. For other examples, consult the list beginning on page 19. The first part of the following list deals with perfectly good words that have been confused. The second part reveals pronunciations resulting in nonexistent, incorrect words.

WORDS CONFUSED IN PRONUNCIATION

1. caliber
   caliper
2. carton
   cartoon
3. casualty
   causality
4. celery
   salary
5. cemetery
   symmetry
6. color
   collar
7. concur
   conquer
8. dinghy
   dingy
9. elicit
   illicit
10. errand
    errant
11. faucet
    forceps
12. finally
    finely
13. gesture
    jester
14. gig
    jig
15. impostor
    imposture
16. minister
    minster
17. pastor
    pasture
18. plantiff
    plaintive
19. relic
    relict
20. sculptor
    sculpture
21. sink
    zinc

22. specie   24. veracity   25. way
    species   voracity   whey
23. tenet
    tenant

	CORRECT	INCORRECT
	corsage (small bouquet)	*corsarge* or *cosarge*
	exercise (physical activity)	*excercise*
	garage (storage place)	*gararge*
	height (distance from bottom to top)	*heighth*
	imagine (to form an idea)	*imangine*
	irrelevant (unrelated)	*irrevelant*
	poem (literary composition)	*pome*
	radio (transmission of sound waves)	*raido* or *radeo*
	research (systematic inquiry)	*reaserch*
	strategic (favorable or advantageous)	*stragetic*
	temperature (degree of heat)	*tempreture*
	third (Number 3 in a series)	*thrid* or *therd*
	tragedy (serious drama or event)	*tradegy*

INCORRECT PREFIXES

You don't transpose or otherwise confuse letters as is done in the list above? Good. The misspellings do look senseless and are characteristic of poor spellers. But you may have difficulty pronouncing and spelling certain words which have prefixes. (A prefix is usually one syllable added to the beginning of a word to alter its meaning or create a new word. The syllable *pre* is itself a prefix meaning "before in time," "earlier than.") Many prefixes were borrowed from Latin and Greek and do cause some people trouble with pronunciation, and hence spelling. Here are a few examples of words beginning with *per*, *pre*, and *pro*, the only prefixes which cause real trouble in pronouncing and spelling English words:

	CORRECT	INCORRECT
	perform (to act, to do)	*preform*
	perhaps (possibly, probably)	*prehaps*
	perjury (breaking an oath)	*prejury*

CORRECT	INCORRECT
perspiration (sweating)	*prespiration*
perversely (persisting in error)	*preversely*
precipitate (to cause action)	*percipitate*
professor (a teacher)	*perfessor* or *prefessor*
proposal (a plan, scheme)	*porposal* or *preprosal*

ADDED VOWELS

Some words are misspelled because in pronouncing them an extra vowel is added. A list of them would not be long, but since many of them are frequently used they merit careful study. Mispronouncing them may cause you not only to misspell but also to be looked on as careless in speech or uneducated, or both.

CORRECT	INCORRECT
athletics (sports, games)	*athaletics* or *atheletics*
disastrous (causing harm, grief)	*disasterous*
entrance (act or point of coming in)	*enterance*
explanation (interpretation)	*explaination*
grievous (serious, grave)	*grievious*
Henry (proper name)	*Henery*
hindrance (obstacle, impediment)	*hinderance*
hundred (the number)	*hundered*
laundry (washing of clothes)	*laundery* or *laundary*
mischievous (prankish)	*mischievious*
monstrous (huge, enormous)	*monsterous*
nervous (emotionally tense)	*nerveous*
partner (associate)	*partener*
remembrance (souvenir, keepsake)	*rememberance*
similar (alike)	*similiar*
Spanish (pertaining to Spain)	*Spainish*
umbrella (shade or screen)	*umberella*

DROPPED VOWELS

There are many different ways to misspell words: you can do so by dropping vowels as well as by adding them. Educated speakers often drop vowels in pronouncing some words in the following list; there-

fore you should study this list carefully since even acceptable pronunciation is not always a sure guide. However, a few of these words
could not be pronounced correctly from the faulty spelling shown—
whole syllables would drop out. Only in highly informal speech or
television advertising would *caramel* be pronounced *carmel*.

1. John's truck accidentally (not *accidently*) hit the child.
2. This is an *auxiliary* (not *auxilary*) gasoline tank.
3. The physician prescribed *beneficial* (not *benefical*) drugs.
4. The pianist gave a *brilliant* (not *brillant*) recital.
5. He is a soldier, not a *civilian* (not *civilan*).
6. This harsh *criticism* (not *critcism*) is merited.
7. She is a *conscientious* (not *conscientous*) housewife.
8. This *convenient* (not *convenent*) room is for your use.
9. John is *deficient* (not *deficent*) in his accounts.
10. Mary is an *efficient* (not *efficent*) typist.
11. Your face is *familiar* (not *familar*).
12. I seek your *financial* (not *financal*) help.
13. King Cole was a merry, *genial* (not *genal*) soul.
14. Beethoven was a man of *genius* (not *genus*).
15. Your sentence is *grammatically* (not *grammaticly*) sound.
16. The money is only *incidentally* (not *incidently*) important.
17. The chemistry *laboratory* (not *labortory*) is large.
18. I like to read good *literature* (not *literture*).
19. *Mathematics* (not *mathmatics*) deals with numbers.
20. A child is a *miniature* (not *minature*) man.
21. Your *opinion* (not *opinon*) is valid.
22. This is an *original* (not *orignal*) idea.
23. Sir Henry is a member of *Parliament* (not *Parliment*).
24. He is *proficient* (not *proficent*) as a manager.
25. Sue has an even *temperament* (not *temperment*).

In addition to these twenty-five words illustrated in sentences, check
your pronunciation of the following. Some people slur over the vowels which are shown in bold face; some omit them entirely; some
pronounce them with considerable stress. Pronounce each word as
you normally do. If the letters in bold face are silent, or lightly stressed
in your speech, you are likely to omit them from your spelling.

accompan**i**ment	asp**i**rin	bound**a**ry
acc**u**racy	bach**e**lor	cas**u**alties

considerable   ignorant   operate
criminal   lengthening   particular
definite   liable   privilege
delivery   luxury   regular
different   magazine   scenery
family   memory   similar
frivolous   misery   temperature
history   Niagara   victory

DROPPED CONSONANTS

As we have noticed, spelling is definite, fixed, and unyielding. But not so with pronunciation, since that is constantly changing, differs from place to place, and is even varied on different occasions by the same speaker. The word *garden* is always spelled g-a-r-d-e-n, but it can be, and is, pronounced in half a dozen different ways. You can drop the *r* or retain it. You can use any of three different sounds for the two vowels in the word, with or without shadings of sound. Each of these pronunciations is correct and normally is completely understood when used.

Such variation in pronouncing words sometimes does cause spelling problems. If our visual memory of words is stronger than our auditory image, no harm is done. But when a letter is incorrectly omitted in pronouncing a word, we have to be on guard. The following representative list of words should be studied carefully. If you master this list, you will then be alert to still other words in which consonants are slurred over or remain silent. In each word the "offending" consonant is set in bold face; try to pronounce it fully, sounding it out as an aid to your auditory memory.

1. Mr. Avery is an old ac**q**uaintance of mine.
2. The Arc**t**ic Circle is entirely imaginary.
3. This puts me in an awk**w**ard position.
4. He is a candi**d**ate for the office.
5. The driver was convicted of drunken**n**ess.
6. He stopped school in the eig**h**th grade.
7. Mac grew up in a poor enviro**n**ment.
8. Feb**r**uary is the shortest month in the year.
9. He is opposed to all forms of gover**n**ment.

10. Karen is now a proud kin*d*ergarten pupil.
11. He owns a luc*r*ative business.
12. There are thousands of books in her lib*r*ary.
13. The barn was struck by light*n*ing.
14. You are per*h*aps too hasty in judging me.
15. Sam is proba*b*ly the best salesman in the company.
16. He purchased a large quan*t*ity of food.
17. This is a quar*t*er, not a dime.
18. Mae did not seem to reco*g*nize me.
19. He was a good representa*t*ive for the firm.
20. This statement su*r*prised me.

In addition to these twenty illustrated words, and as a start on your additional list, pronounce each of the following as you ordinarily do. Perhaps your pronunciation will offer a clue to the cause of some of your misspellings. In each word, the "offending" consonant appears in bold face. Some of these consonants are silent or are slurred over.

accep*t*	gran*d*father	reco*g*nize
ac*q*uire	han*d*ful	*rh*eumatism
an*d*	han*d*le	*rh*ythm
authen*t*ic	hus*t*le	slep*t*
colum*n*	iden*t*ical	sof*t*en
condem*n*	kep*t*	swep*t*
consum*p*tion	lan*d*lord	temp*t*
contempt	lis*t*en	ten*t*ative
emp*t*y	nes*t*le	tres*t*le
excep*t*	of*t*en	use*d* to
fas*c*inate	prom*p*t	wres*t*le
fas*t*en	pum*p*kin	yello*w*

UNSTRESSED VOWELS

No words in English are more often misspelled than those which contain unstressed (or lightly stressed) vowels. An unstressed vowel, like the *a* in *dollar,* is uttered with little force; its sound is faint, indistinct, blurred.

A technical name, *schwa* (ə), is used to indicate this sound of unstressed vowels. It resembles a kind of "uh," a quiet sound much less vigorous than the stronger "uh" sound found in such words as *mud* and *rush*.

This unstressed vowel sound may be represented in spelling by any one of the letters: *a, e, i, o, u*.

a: gramm*a*r, sof*a*, *a*bove   **o:** profess*o*r, spons*o*r, *o*ccur
e: corn*e*r, mod*e*l, *e*stablish   **u:** murm*u*r, sulf*u*r, lux*u*ry
i: nad*i*r, per*i*l, or*i*gin

The letter *y* is sometimes a vowel also. Its unstressed sound is illustrated in the word *martyr*.

Although the schwa sound ("uh") is the most frequent unstressed vowel sound, it is not the only one. An unstressed *i* sound appears in such words as *solid* but is not always spelled as *i*. Note, for example, such words as priv*a*te, privil*e*ge. Still other unstressed vowel sounds occur in American speech, but isolating them is not helpful in learning to spell.

Unless both your auditory and visual memory are excellent, you must be suspicious of words containing lightly stressed syllables. It may help to exaggerate the "trouble spots" when you pronounce such words. Doing so may result in strained or even incorrect pronunciation, but you will increase your auditory image of words which, by sound alone, could be spelled in various ways. If the word *separate*, for example, causes you trouble, pronounce it "sep-A-rate" until you have its spelling firmly fixed in your visual, auditory, and motor images. Here is a representative list of sixty words often misspelled because of the unstressed vowels they contain:

academy	corner	fakir
accident	democracy	grammar
actor	describe	hangar
applicant	despair	humorous
arithmetic	develop	hunger
benefit	dilute	hypocrisy
business	discipline	loafer
calendar	distress	luxury
category	dollar	maintenance
clamor	ecstasy	martyr
comparative	excellent	mathematics
competitive	existence	medicine

model	politics	ridiculous
monastery	possible	separate
murmur	private	sofa
nadir	privilege	solid
occur	professor	sponsor
optimism	propaganda	swindler
origin	repetition	terror
peril	respectable	vulgar

SILENT LETTERS

Some spelling authorities believe that the single greatest cause of misspelling connected with pronunciation is the silent letter. Sounds have been dropping out of our language for many centuries, but their disappearance has affected pronunciation much more than spelling. Actually, many letters no longer pronounced in certain words persist in our spelling, for no good reason: the *l* in such words as *could, would,* and *should* has been silent for hundreds of years, but it hangs on in spelling.

The problem is compounded when we realize that the majority of the letters in our alphabet appear as silent letters in one word or another:

de*a*d	*h*onest	ras*p*berry
dou*b*t	wei*r*d	of*t*en
s*c*ene	*k*nife	g*u*ess
han*d*some	sa*l*mon	answ*e*r
com*e*	*m*nemonics	yac*h*t
of*f*	colum*n*	bou*gh*
si*g*n	fam*ou*s	

Some silent letters cause little difficulty in spelling. If you are "visual minded," you will automatically put a *k* in *knee* or a *g* in *gnat*. But other letters which are silent, or are so lightly sounded as to be almost unheard, do cause trouble. Here is a list of some common words which, in the pronunciation of most educated people, contain silent letters:

align	bomb	condemn
benign	comb	crumb

daughter	knave	psalm
dough	knee	psychology
dumb	kneel	through
eight	knit	thumb
fourth	knob	tomb
ghastly	knock	womb
ghost	knot	wrap
gnash	know	wreck
gnat	knuckle	wrench
gnaw	plumber	wretch
hymn	pneumatic	wring
indebted	pneumonia	write
knack	prompt	

Once again, pronunciation is not a safe guide to spelling. But *faulty* pronunciation sometimes adds hazards. Pronouncing words correctly is at least a slight aid in correct spelling. Try to form clear and definite *auditory* and *visual* images of words whose pronunciation can compound spelling problems.

Here is a final list of words the careless pronunciation of which may cause misspellings. A few words in this list have been covered earlier in this chapter, but repetition may be useful.

accep (for *accept*)
accidently (for *accidentally*)
acrost (for *across*)
asprin (for *aspirin*)
atakt (for *attack*)
athaletics (for *athletics*)
attackted (for *attacked*)
carmel (for *caramel*)
cartoon (for *carton*)
colyum (for *column*)
congradulate (for *congratulate*)
defnite (for *definite*)
dintcha (for *didn't you*)
disasterous (for *disastrous*)
distrik (for *district*)
doncha (for *don't you*)
drownded (for *drowned*)

envirament (for *environment*)
excep (for *except*)
famly (for *family*)
feller (for *fellow*)
finely (for *finally*)
gennelman (for *gentleman*)
gonna (for *going to*)
grievious (for *grievous*)
havncha (for *haven't you*)
hinderance (for *hindrance*)
histry (for *history*)
hundered (for *hundred*)
hyt-th (for *height*)
idenical (for *identical*)
incidently (for *incidentally*)
innerference (for *interference*)
inny (for *any*)

izda (for *is the*)

jester (for *gesture*)

jool (for *jewel*)

kep (for *kept*)

kintergarden
(for *kindergarten*)

krool (for *cruel*)

laundery (for *laundry*)

literture (for *literature*)

mischievious (for *mischievous*)

modren (for *modern*)

monsterous (for *monstrous*)

nukular (for *nuclear*)

porpose (for *propose*)

practicly (for *practically*)

preform (for *perform*)

pressdent (for *president*)

probly (for *probably*)

progidy (for *prodigy*)

reaserch (for *research*)

reconize (for *recognize*)

rememberance
(for *remembrance*)

represenative
(for *representative*)

sawr (for *saw*)

shudder (for *shutter*)

similiar (for *similar*)

slep (for *slept*)

smothertam
(for *some other time*)

strenth (for *strength*)

suprise (for *surprise*)

tempature (for *temperature*)

tempermental
(for *temperamental*)

tradegy (for *tragedy*)

tremenjous (for *tremendous*)

umberella (for *umbrella*)

use to (for *used to*)

vallable (for *valuable*)

victry (for *victory*)

walkin (for *walking*)

wanna (for *want to*)

whachusay (for *what you say*)

whosit (for *who's it*)

willya (for *will you*)

wozzat (for *what's that*)

wunnerful (for *wonderful*)

wunst (for *once*)

youman (for *human*)

zat (for *that*)

5

USE A DICTIONARY: ETYMOLOGY

When you are suspicious of the spelling of any word you should check it immediately in your dictionary. "Doubt + dictionary = good spelling" is a reliable formula. However, it is a counsel of perfection, one that few of us are likely always to follow. Not only that, our sense of doubt may be so great that we spend half our writing time flipping dictionary pages rather than communicating and thus grow bored and frustrated.

Also, you may have tried to look up a word in the dictionary and been unable to find it. If your visual image of a word is weak, you can frustrate yourself even more: look for *agast* and you may give up before discovering that the word is *aghast*. You won't find *pharmacy* and *photograph* among words beginning with *f*. In fact, the confusion of sound and spelling has caused more than one reputable publishing firm seriously to consider preparing a dictionary for poor spellers. Such a dictionary would have been helpful to the man who was away on a trip and telephoned his secretary to send his gun to him at a hunting resort. The secretary could barely hear him (the connection was poor) and asked her boss to spell out what he wanted. "Gun," he shouted. "*G* as in *Jerusalem*, *u* as in *Europe*, *n* as in *pneumonia*." Whether or not he received his *jep* is unknown; maybe she sent him a dictionary instead.

THE DICTIONARY AS AN AID IN SPELLING

Even top-notch spellers consult a dictionary for the spelling of some words. You may not hesitate over *chiaroscuro* or *chimerical*, but you may need to look up *aficionado* or *solipsism* or *Yggdrasil*. Granting that few of us would use these words in the first place, most of us would check our doubts by consulting a dictionary each time. In addition, compound words frequently require hyphens for correct spelling; even superb spellers must look up many such words.

If you haven't done so yet, now would be a good time to get thoroughly acquainted with your dictionary. Better still, make it your friend; best of all, make it your constant companion. To paraphrase the words of Dr. Samuel Johnson, a great dictionary-maker, you would be well advised to give your days and nights to wise study of your dictionary.

CHOICE OF A DICTIONARY

But you should know that there are dictionaries and dictionaries. Some, such as a pocket dictionary, are so small as to be virtually worthless save as a limited guide to spelling and pronunciation. Others, of fair size, may have been so hastily and carelessly produced that they are unreliable. Even the name "Webster" is no longer a guarantee of quality because as a label "Webster" is no longer copyrighted and appears alike in the titles of both reliable and unreliable dictionaries. You should have—and if you don't have, you should buy—a dictionary you can trust.

Suitable dictionaries are what economists refer to as "durable goods." It is well worth paying a few dollars to buy a good, hardbound dictionary that you can keep and use for many years. Equip yourself with a sufficiently large dictionary (approximately 100,000 entries), published by a reliable firm. These, for example, are good dictionaries:

The American Heritage Dictionary of the English Language
Funk & Wagnalls Standard College Dictionary
The Random House Dictionary of the English Language
Webster's New Collegiate Dictionary
Webster's New World Dictionary of the American Language

WORD DERIVATION AND SPELLING

Etymology, a word taken from Greek, means an account of the history of a given word. More particularly, etymology deals with the origin and derivation of words. Knowing what a word comes from will often help you to spell it correctly. For example, the word *preparation* is derived from the Latin prefix *prae* ("beforehand") plus *parare* (meaning "to make ready"). Knowing this, and accenting the first *a* in *parare*, may help you to spell the word correctly: preparation, not preperation.

Similarly, our word *dormitory* (a building containing sleeping rooms) is derived from the Latin word *dormitorium*. Noting the first *i* in this Latin word, and perhaps also knowing that the French word for sleep is *dormir*, may help you to spell *dormitory* with an *i* and not an *a*.

A study of etymology primarily will aid one in building a vocabulary. But it also has its uses in learning to spell. Here are simplified comments on a few other common words which may fix this principle in your mind and lead to further study:

1. *Atmosphere.* This word meaning "the air," "the gaseous envelope surrounding the earth," is made from a learned borrowing from Greek, *atmo,* meaning "air," and *sphere,* meaning "a rounded body." Thus, *atmosphere* literally means "the earth's air."

2. *Biography.* The written account of another person's life is composed of *bio,* a prefix meaning "life," and *graphy,* a combining form denoting some process or form of writing, drawing, or representing.

3. *Calendar.* This word is descended from the Latin word for "account book," *calendarium.* Note the *a;* we frequently misspell the word as *calender* (a perfectly good word with an entirely different meaning).

4. *Consensus.* This word comes from the same Latin root as *consent* (*con* + *sentire,* to feel). Note the *s* in *sentire* and you will not spell the word *concensus,* as is frequently done.

5. *Denim.* This heavy twill cotton material takes its name from *Nimes,* a city in France.

6. *Equivalent.* This frequently misspelled word may be easier for you if you remember that it means "equal in value" and is derived from the prefix *equi* + *valere.* Accent the *val* sound in *valere* (value).

7. *Extravagance.* This word is composed of *extra* (beyond) plus the Latin word *vagans* (*vagari,* to wander). "Extravagance" is wandering beyond limits. Accent the letters *v-a-g* in the root word to insure correct spelling.

8. *Familiar.* This common word, often misspelled with an *e* where the second *a* should appear, is related to the Latin word *familia* (servants in a household).

9. *Finis.* This synonym for "end" has the same origin as the words *definite* and *finite.* Accent the *i* sound and come up with two *i*'s in this word.

10. *Medicine.* Many people tend to spell the second syllable of this word with an *e.* Its origin goes back to Latin *medicina* (*medicus*). Accent the *i* as an aid to correct spelling.

11. *Optimism.* This word comes to us by way of the French word *optimisme* (from Latin *optimus,* meaning "best"). Focus on the two *i*'s in *optimism.*

12. *Privilege.* From *privus* (private) plus *lex, legis* (law), this word can be remembered as "privy" (private) with the *y* changing to *i* plus *legal,* which fixes *leg* in *privilege.*

13. *Prologue.* Meaning a preliminary discourse or preface, this word is formed from a prefix meaning "before" and *logue,* a combining form denoting a spoken or written statement.

14. *Recommend.* This word comes from Latin *recommendare.* Think of it as *re + commend* and avoid that too-often-present double *c.*

15. *Sandwich.* This word owes its existence to the Earl of Sandwich (1718–1792) who was so fond of the gaming table that he refused to stop gambling for regular meals and instead ate bread with fillings of meat or fish. Remember that Sandwich was a gambler, not a witch, and thus avoid the misspelling *sandwitch.* (Or maybe you would like to be able to eat a sandwich in the tropical Sandwich Islands, the former name for the Hawaiian Islands?)

16. *Sentiment.* This word derives from Latin *sentire,* meaning "to feel," "to perceive." Note the *i* in *sentire* and thus spell the word *sentiment.*

17. *Sophomore.* This word comes from the Greek word *sophos,* meaning "wise," and *moros,* meaning "foolish." There seem to be enough *o*'s in the original words to help us remember that we spell this word for "wise fool" as *sophomore.*

18. *Television.* *Tele* is a learned borrowing from Greek, meaning "distant." *Vision* means "sight." *Television* therefore means "distant sight," "seeing from afar."

19. *Thermostat.* This word comes from a Greek word, *thermos,* meaning "hot," plus another Greek word meaning "stationary." Remember the *o* in *thermos* and spell the word "thermostat."

20. *Unanimous.* This word comes from Latin *unus,* meaning "one," plus *animus,* meaning "mind." Our word begins with the first

syllable of *unus* and the first two syllables of *animus:* unani-. Now you will just have to remember to insert an *o* to come up with *unanimous.*

As a beginning for your list of words the origin of which may help you with spelling, consult a good dictionary for the derivations of the following:

1. addict	8. dictaphone	15. monotone
2. amorphous	9. epilogue	16. pantomime
3. assess	10. exhilarate	17. photograph
4. astronomy	11. genesis	18. professor
5. atheist	12. hypodermic	19. recognize
6. auditorium	13. interdict	20. resemblance
7. boycott	14. kindergarten	

A considerable number of the memory devices beginning on page 119 are based upon etymology. Study them now or, when you come to them, refer again to this chapter.

USE A DICTIONARY: PREFIXES, SUFFIXES, AND COMBINING FORMS

Prefixes, as we have noted, are syllables added to the beginning of words to alter or modify their meaning or, occasionally, to form entirely new words. For example, we add the prefix *mis-* to the word *spell* and form *misspell.*

Suffixes are syllables added at the end of words to alter their meanings, to form new words, or to show grammatical function (part of speech). Thus we add *-ish* to *small* and form *smallish.*

Combining form is a term for a word element that rarely appears independently but forms part of a longer word. For instance, *-graph* is a combining form that appears in such words as *photograph* and *lithography.* Knowing the meanings of such forms will help in increasing one's vocabulary and in spelling.

The readiness with which prefixes and suffixes are tacked on to root words in the English language is an indication of the freedom in word formation that has characterized our language for many centuries. For example, consider the word *recession.* This is derived from a Latin word *cedere* (*cessus*), which has the general meaning of "go." To this base we add the prefix *re-*, which has a generalized meaning of "back" or "again," and the suffix *-ion,* an ending which shows that the word is a noun (name of something).

Related to *recession* are many words with still other prefixes and suffixes but all coming from a similar root, or base: *recede, recess, recessive,* etc. The same root appears in *concession, procession, secession,* etc. The prefix of *recession* occurs in such words as *reception* and *relation.* Examples like this could be extended indefinitely.

For one final example, you can select the root word *scribe* (derived from the Latin equivalent of "to write"). From this root, you can easily form well-known words by using prefixes and suffixes:

ascribe, ascription	describe, description
circumscribe, circumscription	inscribe, inscription

prescribe, prescription   subscribe, subscription
proscribe, proscription   transcribe, transcription

A knowledge of the ways in which prefixes, suffixes, and combining forms are added to words will not only increase your vocabulary but also improve your spelling. However, we shall discuss here only a few common prefixes, suffixes, and combining forms appearing in everyday words. Those interested in these additions to words can consult any of a number of lengthy studies available in almost any library.

PREFIXES

a-	not	amoral, anonymous
ad-	to, against	adverse, adjective
ambi-	around, both	ambiguous, ambidextrous
ante-	before	antedate, anteroom
anti-	opposite	antisocial, antiwar
audio-	hearing	audiovisual, audition
auto-	self, same	autograph, autobiography
bene-	well, good	beneficial, benefit
bio-	life	biography, biology
circum-	about, around	circumstance, circumflex
co-	complement of	comaker, co-signer
col-	together	collateral, collection
com-	in association	combine, compare
de-	away, down, from	demerit, degrade
dis-	apart, not, away	disbar, disability
ec- (ex-)	from, out of	eccentric, exhale
en- (em-)	in, on, into	enact, empower
epi-	upon, before	epigram, epilogue
ex-	out of, from	exclaim, excommunicate
extra-	beyond, without	extrajudicial, extrasensory
hemi-	half	hemisphere, hemiplegia
hyper-	beyond the ordinary	hypercritical, hypersensitive
il-	not	illogical, illegitimate
im-	opposed, negative	immoral, imbalance
inter-	among, between	interdepartmental, intercollegiate
intra-	within	intramural, intravenous

ir-	not, opposed	irreligious, irreducible
meta-	along with, among	metaphysics, metamorphism
mono-	one, alone	monochrome, monologue
neo-	new, recent	neophyte, neolithic
para-	beside	paragraph, parachute
per-	through, thoroughly	pervert, perfect
peri-	about, beyond	perimeter, perigee
poly-	marry	polygon, polysyllable
post-	behind, after	postscript, postgraduate
pro-	for, forward	proclivity, proceed
pseudo-	false	pseudoclassic, pseudonym
re-	backward, again	revert, return
retro-	backward	retrogress, retroactive
semi-	half	semidetached, semicolon
super-	above, beyond	supernatural, supersensitive
syn-	together, with	synthesis, syndrome
tel- (tele-)	distant	telegraph, telecast
trans-	across, beyond	transcend, transmit
ultra-	beyond, in excess of	ultraviolet, ultrasonic
un-	not, reverse of	unfair, unbend

This is a brief list of prefixes, but they appear in a large number of misspelled words. Here are notes on the spelling of words containing a few of these prefixes:

Ad-

This prefix alters its form according to the root word to which it is attached. For example, before a root beginning *sc* or *sp*, the *d* is dropped, as in *ascent* and *aspire*. Before such letters as *c, f, g, l, n, p,* and *t*, the *d* in *ad-* is assimilated (becomes the same as the following letter): *accommodate, affix, aggression, allegation, announce, appoint, attend*.

Ante-, anti-

The first of these prefixes is of Latin origin and means "before" or "prior." *Anti-* is from Greek and means "opposite" or "against." Note these different spellings:

*ante*bellum (before the war)
*ante*meridian (before noon; A.M.)
ante mortem (before death)

*ante*room (room before)
*ante*type (an earlier form)
*anti*aircraft (defense against aircraft)
*anti*biotic (defense against bacteria)
*anti*climax (contrast to preceding rise in action)
*anti*freeze (against freezing)
*anti*septic (against infection)

De-, dis-

These prefixes will cause spelling problems when you don't distinguish clearly between root words beginning with *s* and the prefixes themselves. Note these spellings:

describe (write down) *de + scribe*
despoil (strip down) *de + spoil*
dissemble (disguise) *dis + semble*
dissimilar (unlike) *dis + similar*

Remember: only about thirty common words begin with *diss-* but ten times as many begin with *dis-*. Only three fairly common words (and their derivatives) begin with *dys-*: *dysentery, dyspepsia, dystrophy* (as in "muscular dystrophy").

A simple rule: when the prefixes *dis-* and *mis-* are added to a *root* word beginning with *s*, neither *s* should be omitted: *dissatisfied, misstep.* When they are added to roots not beginning with an *s*, use only one *s*: *disappear, misfortune.*

Inter-

This prefix meaning "between" is frequently confused with *intra-*, which means "inside," "within."

interfere (carry between)
intercollegiate (between colleges)
interstate (between, among states)
intramural (within the walls)
intrastate (within a state)
intravenous (within a vein, veins)

Un-

When this prefix is added to a root word beginning with *n*, neither *n* is omitted:

unnamed	unnegotiable	unnumbered
unnatural	unnoted	unnurtured
unnecessary	unnoticeable	
unneeded	unnoticed	

SUFFIXES

As has been indicated, a suffix is an element that is placed after a word or word root to make a term of different use or meaning. For example, the suffix *-age* has a general meaning of "belonging to." *Postage* (*post* plus *age*) has to do with a series of stations along a route that receive and send mail. With this sense of *-age* in mind, words such as *coinage, fruitage, spoilage,* and *bondage* become clear. Common suffixes include these:

-ana	Americana, collegiana	*-let*	bracelet, ringlet
-ance	connivance, nonchalance	*-like*	lifelike, childlike
-dom	kingdom, freedom	*-logy*	trilogy, theology
-er	loiterer, embezzler	*-ness*	kindness, preparedness
-fold	manifold, twofold	*-phone*	telephone, megaphone
-ful	beautiful, harmful	*-polis*	metropolis, megalopolis
-graph	monograph, lithograph	*-ship*	friendship, statesmanship
-hood	childhood, priesthood	*-some*	twosome, quarrelsome
-ice	apprentice, novice	*-ward*	toward, afterward
-ish	British, girlish	*-ways*	always, sideways
-ism	barbarism, plagiarism	*-wise*	clockwise, sidewise
-ity	civility, nobility	*-y*	dreamy, infamy

There are only eight suffix groups which cause major spelling problems. Within each group are many words that give trouble, some of the most often misspelled words in the language. Here is a brief discussion of each of the eight groups.

-Able, -Ible

Even excellent spellers have occasional difficulties with these endings; they can unhesitatingly spell most words having one or the other of these suffixes but once in a while they, too, must seek out their dictionaries.

With this spelling problem the best advice is to "Stop and Look." (It won't do any good to "listen," for pronunciation is identical.) To an efficient speller a word which should end in *-ible* doesn't "look right" when it ends in *-able.* He is relying entirely on his visual image of the correct spelling.

But for those whose visual recall is deficient, there *are* some guiding principles concerning *-able* and *-ible.* They are fairly easy to learn and involve no more exceptions than most rules for spelling. There are five group forms for *-able,* the same number for *-ible.*

-Able

1. The ending should usually be *-able* if the base (root) is a full word: *eat + able.*

Fortunately, many of our most familiar, most used words add *-able* to form adjectives. Note that if you drop *-able* from each of the following you are left with a *complete* word:

acceptable	dependable	peaceable
available	detectable	perishable
avoidable	detestable	predictable
breakable	discreditable	presentable
changeable	drinkable	profitable
comfortable	fashionable	readable
commendable	favorable	seasonable
companionable	laughable	taxable
considerable	noticeable	thinkable
creditable	passable	workable

2. The ending should usually be *-able* if the base is a full word except for lacking a final *e: desire + able = desirable.*

Fortunately, this group of *-able* words is not nearly so large as the preceding one. The following words illustrate the basic principle:

believable	excitable	presumable
debatable	excusable	sizable
deplorable	likable	usable
describable	lovable	valuable
desirable	pleasurable	

3. The ending should usually be *-able* if the base ends in *i* (the original word may have ended in *y*): *enviable.*

This principle of spelling makes more sense than most spelling "rules." If it were not followed we would have a double *i* (*ii*), an unusual combination even in our weird spelling system.

appreciable	enviable	satisfiable
classifiable	justifiable	sociable
dutiable	reliable	

4. The ending should usually be *-able* if the base has other forms with the sound of long *a: demonstrate, demonstrable.*

This principle will be helpful only if you actually sound out another form (or forms) of the root word to see whether it has (or they have) the long *a* sound: *abominate, abominable; estimate, estimable,* etc.

delectable	inflammable	inviolable
durable	inimitable	irreparable
flammable	innumerable	irritable
impenetrable	inseparable	reparable
impregnable	intolerable	

5. The ending should usually be *-able* if the base ends in hard *c* or hard *g.*

Hard *c* is sounded like the *c* in *cat;* hard *g* has the sound of *g* in *get.* The following words illustrate this principle:

amicable	implacable	irrevocable
applicable	indefatigable	revocable
despicable	navigable	
explicable	practicable	

These five principles cover most of the fairly common words which have endings in *-able.* But there are a few exceptions. If you wish to be able to spell all words ending with *-able,* then study the following by some other method suggested in this book; rules won't help much:

affable	formidable	inscrutable
arable	indomitable	insuperable
culpable	ineffable	malleable
equitable	inevitable	memorable

palpable	potable	unconscionable
portable	probable	vulnerable

-Ible

1. The ending should usually be *-ible* if the base is *not* a full word.

Contrast this principle with Number 1 under *-Able* (above). If the base is a complete word, we then add *-able: mail + able = mailable.* If the base is not a complete word, we add *-ible: ris + ible = risible,* and *poss + ible = possible.*

audible	feasible	negligible
combustible	horrible	ostensible
compatible	incorrigible	plausible
credible	indelible	tangible
dirigible	infallible	terrible
divisible	intelligible	visible
edible	irascible	

2. The ending should usually be *-ible* if the base ends in *-ns. respons + ible = responsible.*

These words illustrate this spelling principle:

comprehensible	insensible	responsible
defensible	irresponsible	sensible
incomprehensible	ostensible	
indefensible	reprehensible	

3. The ending should usually be *-ible* if the base ends in *-miss: admiss + ible = admissible.*

Comparatively few words belong in this category. Here are several examples:

dismissible	permissible	transmissible
omissible	remissible	

With roots not ending in *-miss,* but closely related, are such words with *-ible* endings as *accessible, compressible, irrepressible,* and *possible* (which also fits under Group 1 above).

4. The ending should usually be *-ible* if *-ion* can be added to the base without intervening letters: *collect, collection, collectible.*

Quite a few words create such new forms by the immediate (nothing coming between) addition of *-ion*. All such words form adjectives ending in *-ible;* here are a few samples:

accessible	contractible	inexhaustible
affectible	convertible	perfectible
collectible	corruptible	reversible
connectible	digestible	suggestible

You should note that this rule is tricky: if *-ion* cannot be added to the root immediately (without intervening letters), the *-able* ending is more likely as in *present, presentation, presentable.*

5. The ending should usually be *-ible* if the base ends in soft *c* or soft *g.*

This principle should be compared with Number 5 under *-Able.* A soft *c* sounds like an *s* (force); a soft *g* sounds like a *j* (tangent). The following words contain a soft *c* or a soft *g.* Also note that, with few exceptions, the roots are not complete words.

conducible	incorrigible	negligible
convincible	intangible	producible
deducible	intelligible	reducible
eligible	invincible	seducible
forcible	irascible	
illegible	legible	

Just as there are a few exceptions to the rules for *-able* endings (see page 67) so are there for words ending in *-ible.* The commonly used words which are exceptions are not numerous. Among those words which, by rule, should end in *-able* but do not are the following:

collapsible	flexible	irresistible
contemptible	gullible	resistible
discernible	inflexible	

The following words merit careful study because each is an exception to the principles discussed above:

correctable	dispensable	predictable
detectable	indispensable	

-Ally, -Ly

These two suffixes are often confused by spellers with inadequate visual memories. Because these endings appear so often in commonly used words, they account for large numbers of misspellings. The same advice applies: when in doubt, consult your dictionary.

Perhaps these basic principles concerning -ly will also be helpful:

1. The suffix -ly is used to form an adverb from an adjective: *poor + ly = poorly*. If the adjective ends in -l, -ly is tacked on to the complete root, thus producing an -lly ending.

Here is a list of frequently used, and occasionally misspelled, adverbs:

accidentally	fundamentally	personally
actually	generally	physically
annually	incidentally	practically
continually	individually	really
coolly	intentionally	skillfully
cruelly	literally	successfully
especially	logically	truthfully
exceptionally	morally	universally
finally	naturally	unusually
fully	occasionally	usually

2. The suffix -ly is added to basic words ending in silent *e*, and the *e* is retained.

absolutely	immediately	severely
completely	infinitely	sincerely
entirely	scarcely	

3. If an adjective ends in -ic, its adverbial form ends in -ally.

This is a simple, clear rule with only one exception: *publicly*. This word you must simply fix in your visual memory. Here are examples of adverbs formed from adjectives with -ic endings:

academically	emphatically	scholastically
artistically	fantastically	systematically
automatically	grammatically	
basically	lyrically	

The following adverbs do not completely follow the principles just enumerated. Fix them in your visual memory:

duly	possibly	wholly
incredibly	terribly	
only	truly	

-Ance, -Ence

The suffixes *-ance* and *-ence* are added to root words (verbs) to form nouns: *attend, attendance; prefer, preference.*

With one exception, to be noted below, there is no uniform guiding principle to your choice of *-ance* or *-ence.* Here again, correct pronunciation is of no help. True, if you know the conjugation of Latin verbs you can form a helpful rule, but so few of us do know Latin that it's useless to state the principle. Your only safe procedure is to consult your dictionary and try to form good visual images of *-ance* and *-ence* words.

One helpful principle, and one only, is this: if a verb ends in *r* preceded by a vowel and is accented on the last syllable, it forms its noun with *-ence:*

abhorrence	deference	preference
coherence	inference	recurrence
concurrence	interference	reference
conference	occurrence	transference

Here are lists of often misspelled words ending in *-ance* and *-ence.* Study each until you have a total recall of its appearance.

FREQUENTLY MISSPELLED *-ANCE* WORDS

abeyance	appearance	distance
abundance	arrogance	elegance
acceptance	assurance	endurance
acquaintance	attendance	entrance
admittance	balance	furtherance
allegiance	brilliance	grievance
alliance	continuance	guidance
allowance	contrivance	instance
ambulance	defiance	insurance
annoyance	deliverance	irrelevance

FREQUENTLY MISSPELLED -*ANCE* WORDS (*Cont'd*)

maintenance	relevance	significance
nuisance	reliance	substance
observance	remembrance	sustenance
performance	remittance	temperance
perseverance	repentance	tolerance
radiance	resistance	vengeance

FREQUENTLY MISSPELLED -*ENCE* WORDS

absence	difference	obedience
abstinence	eminence	patience
audience	essence	permanence
circumference	evidence	preference
coherence	excellence	presence
coincidence	existence	prominence
competence	experience	prudence
conference	impudence	reference
confidence	incidence	residence
conscience	inference	reverence
convenience	influence	sentence
correspondence	innocence	silence
deference	insistence	subsistence
dependence	interference	violence

-*Ar*, -*Er*, -*Or*

The suffixes -*ar*, -*er*, and -*or* have various origins, functions, and meanings. Their most common shared meaning denotes an actor, a doer, "one who." Many thousands of English words end in -*ar*, -*er*, and -*or*, but here again accurate pronunciation is little aid in spelling; furthermore, no rules or principles are applicable to their correct spelling. Consult your dictionary; try to form accurate visual images.

Following are lists of -*ar*, -*er*, and -*or* words often misspelled. In not every word is the ending a true suffix, but correct spelling is now your objective, not a study of word origins or of word building.

FREQUENTLY MISSPELLED WORDS ENDING IN -*AR*

altar	burglar	cedar
angular	calendar	cellar
beggar	caterpillar	circular

collar	lunar	regular
curricular	molar	scholar
dollar	muscular	similar
familiar	nectar	singular
grammar	particular	spectacular
hangar	peculiar	sugar
insular	pillar	vehicular
jugular	polar	vinegar
liar	popular	vulgar

FREQUENTLY MISSPELLED WORDS ENDING IN -ER

advertiser	defender	minister
adviser	diameter	murder
alter	disaster	observer
announcer	employer	officer
baker	examiner	partner
beginner	foreigner	passenger
believer	haberdasher	prisoner
boarder	jeweler	provider
border	laborer	soldier
boulder	lawyer	teacher
carrier	lecturer	traveler
commissioner	manager	writer
consumer	manufacturer	
debater	messenger	

FREQUENTLY MISSPELLED WORDS ENDING IN -OR

accelerator	collector	doctor
actor	commentator	editor
administrator	competitor	educator
aggressor	conqueror	elevator
anchor	contributor	emperor
auditor	councilor	escalator
author	counselor	executor
aviator	creditor	factor
bachelor	debtor	governor
behavior	dictator	harbor
benefactor	director	humor
cantor	distributor	inferior

FREQUENTLY MISSPELLED WORDS ENDING IN -OR (Cont'd)

inventor	neighbor	sculptor
investigator	odor	senator
janitor	pastor	suitor
legislator	prior	supervisor
manor	professor	tenor
minor	protector	traitor
mortgagor	radiator	ventilator
motor	sailor	visitor

-Ary, -Ery

This suffix problem is simple. Hundreds and hundreds of English words end in -*ary*. Only a half dozen fairly common words end in -*ery*. Learn the -*ery* words by whatever device presented in this book works best for you. Spell all others with -*ary*. It's as element*ary* as that.

Here are the words you might use which end in -*ery*:

cemetery	distillery	monastery
confectionery	millinery	stationery

If you're a physician, you probably know how to spell *dysentery*. If you're not a physician, another word, more easily spelled, can and will suffice.

End all other words with -*ary*. You'll be right every time unless you happen to use such a rare word as *philandery*. You will have no spelling problems with the endings of *auxiliary, boundary, dictionary, elementary, honorary, imaginary, library, secretary,* and *voluntary,* and hundreds of other such everyday words.

-Cede, -Ceed, -Sede

These suffixes cause a large number of misspellings because they appear in several common words. But the problem they present is quite simple because so few words are involved. Only twelve words in the language end in this pronunciation, "seed," and not all of these are in common use.

First, only one word in English ends in -*sede: supersede*. It has this ending because of its origin; it comes from the Latin verb *sedeo,* meaning "to sit." As with many other "borrowed" words in English it maintains some connection with its source.

Second, only three of the twelve words ending with the "seed" pronunciation are spelled with *ceed: exceed, proceed,* and *succeed.*

Finally, the eight remaining words end in *cede,* and of these only three or four are in general, everyday use:

accede	concede	recede
antecede	intercede	secede
cede	precede	

It won't help with spelling the *-ceed* and *-cede* words to know their origin, but it will help in avoiding a *sede* ending: the eleven *-ceed,* *-cede* words derive not from *sedeo* (as *supersede* does) but from Latin *cedo,* meaning "to go." Thus, *pre + cede* means "to go or come before"; *inter + cede* means "to go or come between," etc.

-Efy, -Ify

These two suffixes cause much spelling trouble but here again the problem is simple when it is clearly looked at. Actually, only four words you are likely to use end in *-efy* (and you probably won't use them every day, either). All the remainder, without exception, end in *-ify.*

Therefore, learn these four words by whatever method seems best and spell all others with *-ify:*

liquefy (to make liquid)
putrefy (to make or become rotten)
rarefy (to make or become rare)
stupefy (to make or become insensible)

Also, you should note that words built on these four tend to retain the *e* spelling:

liquefy, liquefies, liquefied, liquefying, liquefaction
putrefy, putrefies, putrefied, putrefying, putrefaction
rarefy, rarefies, rarefied, rarefying, rarefaction
stupefy, stupefies, stupefied, stupefying, stupefaction

-Ise, -Ize, -Yze

Some five hundred fairly common words in our language end in *-ise, -ize,* and *-yze.* How can one master all these spellings, especially since correct pronunciation provides no help at all?

Consulting your dictionary will provide some help and so will training your visual memory until a word you've spelled with -ize just "doesn't look right" if it should end in -ise. The best approach is to isolate the comparatively few words with -yze and -ise and to remember that -ize is by far the most common suffix and that the chances of its being correct are mathematically excellent.

These are the only four fairly common words in English ending in -yze and of them you will normally use only two:

analyze	electrolyze
catalyze	paralyze

Study these four words carefully, especially the first and last. Master them by whatever method seems best: four words (or two) are a small matter.

There are no clear rules for choosing between -ise and -ize endings. But although there are well over four hundred words ending in -ize there are only some thirty or forty with an -ise suffix. (If you live in Great Britain, you will have to cope with a larger number; several words that the English spell with -ise Americans spell with -ize.)

The comparatively few words which end in -ise can be grouped as follows:

1. Combinations with -cise:

circumcise	exercise	incise
excise	exorcise	

These -cise words are so spelled because they derive from a form, *incisus,* of a Latin word meaning "to cut."

2. Combinations with -guise:

disguise	guise

3. Combinations with -mise:

compromise	premise
demise	surmise

4. Combinations with *-prise:*

apprise	enterprise	reprise
comprise	emprise	surprise

5. Combinations with *-rise:*

arise	rise	uprise
moonrise	sunrise	

6. Combinations with *-vise:*

advise	improvise	supervise
devise	revise	

These *-vise* words are derived from a form, *visus,* of a Latin word meaning "to see."

7. Combinations with *-wise:*

contrariwise	likewise	sidewise
lengthwise	otherwise	wise

8. Miscellaneous combinations with *-ise:*

advertise	despise	merchandise
chastise	franchise	

This makes a total of less than forty common words ending in *-yze* and *-ise.* All others with this suffixal pronunciation end in *-ize.* Here are a few of the hundreds of words with this ending:

agonize	demoralize	modernize
apologize	economize	monopolize
authorize	equalize	moralize
baptize	familiarize	nationalize
brutalize	fertilize	naturalize
cauterize	generalize	neutralize
characterize	harmonize	organize
Christianize	humanize	ostracize
civilize	jeopardize	particularize
colonize	legalize	pasteurize
criticize	liberalize	patronize
crystallize	localize	philosophize

plagiarize	scandalize	symbolize
pulverize	scrutinize	tantalize
realize	solemnize	utilize
recognize	specialize	vocalize
reorganize	subsidize	

COMBINING FORMS

Learning the meaning and spelling of combining forms will help you in spelling longer words containing them. You can find hundreds of such forms in a good dictionary, but here are a few appearing most often in everyday words.

anima	life, breath	animal, animation
aqua	water	aquarium, aqualung
aristos	the best	aristocrat, aristocracy
beatus	blessed	beatitude, beatification
bios	life	biosphere, biopsy
causa	cause	causal, causation
culpa	fault	culprit, culpable
decem	ten	December, decennial
domus	house	domestic, domicile
ego	I	egoism, egocentric
facilis	easy	facile, facilitate
gramma	letter	grammar, grammatical
hostis	enemy	hostile, hostility
lex	law	legal, legalize
liber	book	library, libretto
locus	place	local, locality
mater	mother	matriarch, maternal
navis	ship	navy, navigate
opus	work	operation, opera
pedi	foot	pedometer, pedicure
petra	rock	petroleum, petrology
plus, pluris	more	plural, plurality
populus	people	population, populate
sanctus	holy	sanctuary, sanctify
sophia	wisdom	sophomore, sophisticated

tacitus	silence	tacit, taciturn
thermo	heat	thermometer, thermal
umbra	shade	umbrella, umbrage
vita	life	vital, vitamin

Use your dictionary to locate the suffixes and combining forms listed below. For each numbered word ending (suffix or combining form) write a letter in the space provided to match it with the term on the right which is a key word or phrase in its dictionary definition.

_____ 1. -androus   a. inferior
_____ 2. -arch   b. male
_____ 3. -ase   c. ancient
_____ 4. -aster   d. decomposes
         e. ruler

_____ 5. -cephalic   a. head
_____ 6. -cide   b. tree
_____ 7. -cracy   c. rule
_____ 8. -dendron   d. kill
         e. judge

_____ 9. -dom   a. becoming
_____ 10. -esce   b. realm
_____ 11. -ese   c. guilty
_____ 12. -fold   d. times
         e. dialect

_____ 13. -gamy   a. woman
_____ 14. -gen   b. walking
_____ 15. -grade   c. producing
_____ 16. -gyny   d. union
         e. evaluation

_____ 17. -hippus   a. medicine
_____ 18. -hood   b. shelter
_____ 19. -iatry   c. whole group
_____ 20. -kin   d. horse
         e. little

_____ 21. -lent　　　a. slender
_____ 22. -ling　　　b. full
_____ 23. -lith　　　c. speaking
_____ 24. -logue　　　d. little
　　　　　　　　　　　e. stone

_____ 25. -lysis　　　a. shape
_____ 26. -mancy　　　b. dissolving
_____ 27. -morph　　　c. divination
_____ 28. -ode　　　d. path
　　　　　　　　　　　e. infesting

_____ 29. -oid　　　a. colored
_____ 30. -pathic　　　b. eating
_____ 31. -petal　　　c. moving toward
_____ 32. -phage　　　d. suffering
　　　　　　　　　　　e. resembling

_____ 33. -phile　　　a. fear
_____ 34. -phobe　　　b. plant
_____ 35. -phyte　　　c. liking
_____ 36. -pod　　　d. foot
　　　　　　　　　　　e. watery

_____ 37. -pter　　　a. condition of
_____ 38. -ship　　　b. tending toward, like
_____ 39. -some　　　c. wing
_____ 40. -stat　　　d. holding steady
　　　　　　　　　　　e. excessive

7

USE A DICTIONARY:
PLURALS

You can consult your dictionary every time you are unsure about the spelling of a word but, as we have noted, if you do you'll be more a whirling dervish or page-flipper than a writer.

Many people find it fairly easy to spell the singular of a word (meaning "one") but have trouble forming and correctly spelling plurals (meaning "more than one"). This is quite understandable, since many English words form plurals in unusual ways. You can "look it up" in a dictionary when you are puzzled, but a few principles of plural-forming can easily be mastered.

NOUN PLURALS

1. The plural of most nouns is formed by adding *s* to the singular:

bed, beds	food, foods
book, books	hat, hats
chair, chairs	pot, pots
cracker, crackers	sheet, sheets
dog, dogs	table, tables

2. Nouns ending with a sibilant or *s* sound (*ch, sh, s, x, z*) form their plurals by adding *es:*

arch, arches	fox, foxes
box, boxes	loss, losses
bush, bushes	mass, masses
buzz, buzzes	tax, taxes
church, churches	watch, watches

3. Nouns ending in *y* preceded by a consonant usually change *y* to *i* before adding *es:*

activity, activities
category, categories
city, cities
community, communities
fly, flies

forty, forties
library, libraries
quantity, quantities
sky, skies
strawberry, strawberries

4. Nouns ending in *y* preceded by a vowel usually add *s* without changing the final *y:*

alley, alleys
attorney, attorneys
chimney, chimneys
foray, forays
key, keys

money, moneys
monkey, monkeys
toy, toys
turkey, turkeys
valley, valleys

5. Nouns ending in *o* preceded by a vowel add *s* to form their plurals:

cameo, cameos
folio, folios

radio, radios
rodeo, rodeos

6. Nouns ending in *o* preceded by a consonant often add *es* to form the plural:

buffalo, buffaloes
cargo, cargoes
echo, echoes
embargo, embargoes
fresco, frescoes
hero, heroes

mosquito, mosquitoes
Negro, Negroes
potato, potatoes
tomato, tomatoes
tornado, tornadoes
volcano, volcanoes

7. Some nouns ending in *o* preceded by a consonant, including many musical terms, add *s* to form their plurals:

alto, altos
banjo, banjos
basso, bassos
canto, cantos
concerto, concertos
contralto, contraltos
dynamo, dynamos
Eskimo, Eskimos

gigolo, gigolos
memento, mementos
piano, pianos
quarto, quartos
silo, silos
solo, solos
soprano, sopranos
zero, zeros

8. Nouns ending in *f* form their plurals in such variable ways that you should *always* consult your dictionary when in doubt. Nouns

ending in *ff* usually add *s*. Most nouns ending in *fe* change *fe* to *ve* and add *s*. The following examples will be sufficient to make you remember the formula: doubt + dictionary = correct spelling:

belief, beliefs	roof, roofs
chief, chiefs	scarf, scarves
fife, fifes	self, selves
grief, griefs	sheaf, sheaves
half, halfs (or halves)	sheriff, sheriffs
handkerchief, handkerchiefs	staff, staves (or staffs)
leaf, leaves	tariff, tariffs
life, lives	thief, thieves
loaf, loaves	wife, wives
mischief, mischiefs	wolf, wolves

COMPOUND NOUNS

9. Compound nouns ordinarily form the plural by adding *s* or *es* to the important word in the compound.

Sometimes the element considered most important comes first in the compound, sometimes at the end. The end element is usually the one pluralized if it and other elements are so closely related as to be considered a single word: *handfuls, housefuls, basketfuls*. Just to confound the pluralizing of compound words, occasionally more than one element is pluralized in the same word. Here again, the best advice is: *Consult your dictionary*. The words listed below illustrate the erratic principles stated in this paragraph:

attorney at law, attorneys at law
attorney general, attorneys general or attorney generals
brother-in-law, brothers-in-law
bystander, bystanders
commander in chief, commanders in chief
consul general, consuls general
father-in-law, fathers-in-law
hanger-on, hangers-on
major general, major generals
master sergeant, master sergeants

manservant, menservants
pailful, pailfuls
passer-by, passers-by
son-in-law, sons-in-law

IRREGULAR PLURALS

10. Some nouns have irregular plurals.

Surely you expected to read the statement above, sooner or later. Here is a representative list of words with plurals that are irregular or plain nonsensical or which follow none of the principles stated above. Try to master them by whatever device you have found most useful:

alkali, alkalies	moose, moose
bison, bison	mouse, mice
brother, brothers, brethren	ox, oxen
child, children	photo, photos
deer, deer	series, series
foot, feet	sheep, sheep
goose, geese	species, species
louse, lice	swine, swine
madam, mesdames	tooth, teeth
man, men	woman, women

11. Pronouns and verbs have plural forms just as do nouns. It is doubtful, however, that misspelling of pronouns is due to their number. If you misspell *their,* a plural pronoun, you are probably confusing *their* and *there,* rather than having trouble with a plural. *We, they, our, us, them,* all plural pronouns, are easy to spell.

   The plurals of verbs are quite simple. Main verbs have the same form for both singular and plural except in the third person singular, present tense: he *sees,* he *moves,* he *thinks,* he *does,* he *goes.* That is, most verbs add an *s* (*es*) in the third person to form a singular. It's easy to remember this: most nouns and verbs form their plurals in directly opposite ways.

NOUNS OF FOREIGN ORIGIN

12. Certain nouns of foreign origin retain the plural of the language from which they were borrowed. Some borrowed words have

gradually assumed plurals with the usual English *s* or *es* endings. Finally, some words have more than one plural form.

To reduce confusion, here is a list of fairly common nouns to fix in your mind by whatever device works best for you:

addendum -da
alumna -nae
alumnus -ni
ameba -bae, -bas
analysis -ses
apparatus -tus, -tuses
appendix -dixes, -dices
automaton -ta, -tons
axis -es
bacillus -li
basis -ses
beau beaus, beaux
cactus -ti, -tuses
chateau -teaus, -teaux
cherub cherubs, cherubim
    (scriptural)
crisis -ses
criterion -ia
curriculum -lums, -la
datum -ta
diagnosis -ses
erratum -ta
focus -ci (scientific), -cuses
    (general)
formula -las, -lae
fungus -gi, -guses
gladiolus -luses, -li
hiatus -tuses, hiatus
hypothesis -ses
index indexes, indices
larva -vae
libretto -tos, -ti

locus loci
madame mesdames
matrix -trixes, -trices
medium -dia, -diums
memorandum -da, -dums
momentum -tums, -ta
monsieur messieurs
moratorium -iums, -ia
nebula -las, -lae
neurosis -ses
nucleus -clei, -cleuses
oasis -ses
opus opera, opuses
ovum -a
parenthesis -ses
psychosis -ses
radius radii, radiuses
rostrum -trums, -tra
species species
stadium -diums, -dia
stimulus -li
stratum -ta, -tums
syllabus -bi, -buses
synopsis -ses
synthesis -ses
tableau -bleaus, -bleaux
terminus -nuses, -ni
thesis -ses
trousseau -seaus, -seaux
vertebra -brae, -bras
vortex -tices, -texes

8
USE A DICTIONARY: APOSTROPHES

An apostrophe is a mark of punctuation, not a letter, and yet when one is improperly added or omitted it causes you to misspell. The apostrophe has several uses, all with some influence on spelling: to indicate the possessive case, to mark omission of letters, to indicate the plurals of letters and numbers. The use of an apostrophe influences both punctuation *and* spelling. Since this book deals only with spelling, we will concentrate on uses of the apostrophe which result in misspelling.

INDICATING POSSESSION

1. Use an apostrophe and *s* to form the possessive case of a noun (singular or plural) not ending in *s:*

children, children's   horse, horse's
doctor, doctor's   town, town's

    Children's shoes are often expensive.

2. Use only an apostrophe to form the possessive case of a plural noun ending in *s:*

boys, boys'   students, students'
ladies, ladies'   weeks, weeks'

    The boys' coats are in the closet.

3. Use an apostrophe alone or an apostrophe with *s* to form the possessive of singular nouns ending in *s:*

Robert Burns, Robert Burns' (or Burns's)
Charles, Charles' (or Charles's)

    She liked Robert Burns' (or Burns's) poetry.
    This is Charles' (or Charles's) hat.

4. In compound nouns add the apostrophe and *s* to the last element of the expression, the one nearest the object possessed:

> my son-in-law's boat   King Henry IV's funeral
> somebody else's ticket   the city manager's salary

INDICATING OMISSION

5. Use an apostrophe to show that letters or figures have been omitted.

> aren't = are not   they're = they are
> don't = do not   wasn't = was not
> he's = he is   weren't = were not

> The Civil War was fought 1861–'65. (1861 to 1865)
> He left home in '59. (1959)

This use of the apostrophe is reflected in the most misspelled short and simple word in the English language. *It's* means "it is" and can never be correctly used for *its* in the possessive sense: "When a dog wags *its* tail, that is a sign *it's* happy." Never write the letters *i-t-s* without asking whether or not you mean "it is."

FORMING PLURALS

6. Use an apostrophe and *s* to indicate the plurals of figures, letters, and words considered as words.

> Small children cannot always make legible 5's.
> Uncrossed *t*'s look like *l*'s.
> He uses too many *and*'s and *but*'s in speaking.

7. Never use an apostrophe in forming the plural of nouns and the possessive case of personal relative pronouns.

> The *Browns* (not *Brown's*) came to see us.

CORRECT	INCORRECT
ours	our's
ours	ours'
yours	your's
yours	yours'

CORRECT	INCORRECT
his	his'
hers	her's
hers	hers'
its	it's
theirs	their's
theirs	theirs'
whose	who's

The apostrophe is essential in the correct spelling of numerous words and expressions. For each numbered part of the following sentences, choose a letter to indicate the preferred spelling.

1. I (*a.* do'nt; *b.* dont; *c.* don't) know
2. (*a.* whose; *b.* who's; *c.* whos') going
3. to win this (*a.* year; *b.* year's; *c.* years'; *d.* years) scholastic award.
4. We met the (*a.* Browns; *b.* Brown's; *c.* Browns') last night
5. at my (*a.* brother-in-law; *b.* brother's-in-law; *c.* brother-in-law's) house.
6. Among all the (*a.* children's; *b.* childrens; *c.* childrens') galoshes parked
7. in the hall, I hardly knew which were (*a.* hers; *b.* her's).
8. The common belief that the Japanese pronounce their (*a. l*'s; *b. l*s'; *c. l*s)
9. to sound like the American *r* (*a.* isnt; *b.* isn't; *c.* is'nt) quite correct;
10. actually (*a.* its; *b.* it's; *c.* its') an intermediate sound not heard in English.
11. Remember that (*a.* anyone else; *b.* anyone's else; *c.* anyone else's; *d.* anyone else')
12. opinion has as good a chance of being right as (*a.* your; *b.* yours; *c.* your's).
13. The (*a.* Jones; *b.* Jones'; *c.* Joneses; *d.* Jones's) telephoned last night to say
14. that (*a.* they're; *b.* their; *c.* there) arriving on Tuesday.
15. It (*a.* can't; *b.* ca'nt; *c.* cant) have been much before

16. twelve (*a.* oclock;   *b.* o'clock;   *c.* o clock) that he came in.

17. For five (*a.* hour;   *b.* hours;   *c.* hour's;   *d.* hours') work

18. (*a.* Jess;   *b.* Jess';   *c.* Jesses;   *d.* Jess's) pay was $18.60.

19. The (*a.* repairmen's;   *b.* repairmens';   *c.* repairmen) demand for a raise in pay

20. was reasonable, but (*a.* its;   *b.* it's) timing was unfortunate.

9

USE A DICTIONARY: COMPOUND WORDS

The centuries-old tendency of the English language to combine words has created still another difficult problem for spellers. Even so, compound words have greatly increased the range and richness of the language and have provided many shortcuts and timesavers.

Now look at the paragraph which you have just read. Note that *centuries-old* is a compound written with a hyphen; that *shortcuts* and *timesavers* are compounds written as one word (no hyphen, no separation). Any one of these words written otherwise would be misspelled.

There are no rules or principles covering *all* combinations. Some few principles, easily learned, are discussed below, but for spelling the bulk of compound words you must use your dictionary whenever you are in doubt.

PRINCIPLES OF WORD JOINING

The general principle of word joining derives from actual usage. When two (or more) words first become associated with a single meaning, they are written separately. As they grow, through usage, to become more of a unit in thought and writing, they are usually hyphenated (spelled with a hyphen). Finally, they tend to be spelled as one word. This evolution may be seen in the following, the third word in each series now being the accepted form: *base ball, base-ball, baseball; rail road, rail-road, railroad.* This general principle, however, is not always in operation; many common expressions which one might think in the third stage are still in the first: *mother tongue, girl scout, in fact, high school.*

Here is another way to demonstrate how seemingly illogical is the spelling of many compound words: look up in your dictionary some of the words which have *red* as the first part of the compound. Dictionaries differ among themselves, but the one the author consulted shows these distinctions: *red cedar, red cent, red clover, Red Cross, red deer, red light, red man, red oak, red pepper, red rose,* and *red tape; red-blooded, red-headed, red-hot,* and *red-letter; redbud, redcap, redcoat, redhead, redwing,* and *redwood.*

The hyphenated *red* words above offer a clue. The hyphen is a device to separate and also a mark to unify, to join. As a mark of spelling, it both joins and separates two or more words used *as an adjective.* And yet it may or may not be called for in forming compound adjectives because of position in a given sentence. For example, hyphens are generally used between the parts of an adjective preceding the substantive (noun) which it modifies but may properly be omitted if the compound adjective follows. You may write "He saw the *red-hot* coil" and just as correctly write "The coil was *red hot.*" Since this is a book on spelling, not syntax, this illustration will have to serve as a warning and as a further plea for you to "look it up" whenever you are doubtful. But remember that dictionaries differ; they do not always indicate the distinction just made.

Finally, you should note that two or more words compounded may have a meaning quite different from that of the same two words not really joined:

Jim was a *battle-scarred* veteran.
The *battle scarred* the body and soul of Jim.
In this quarrel Sue served as a *go-between.*
The ball must *go between* the goal posts.

There is neither a short cut nor an all-inclusive rule for spelling compound words. But perhaps it will be of some help to remember that the present-day tendency is to avoid the use of hyphens whenever possible.

SEVEN CLASSES OF COMPOUND WORDS

There are seven groups, or classes, of compound words with which the hyphen is used:

1. Two or more words modifying a substantive and used as a single adjective.

The hyphen is especially needed in combinations placed *before* the word modified. Examples of these combinations are:

a. adjective, noun, or adverb + participle (+ noun)
Bob is a *sad-looking* boy.
Bell-shaped hats are in fashion again.
He jumped from a *fast-moving* train.

b. adjective + adjective (+ noun)
Mary has *bluish-gray* eyes.

c. adjective + noun (+ noun)
He is a *first-rate* musician.

d. noun + adjective (+ noun)
There will be a *city-wide* search for the criminal.

e. prefix + capitalized adjective (+ noun)
We took a *trans-Andean* clipper to Chile.

The following are other instances of the combinations mentioned above:

able-bodied	loose-tongued
above-mentioned	midnight-black
absent-minded	ocean-blue
Anglo-Saxon	rose-red
best-known	six-room
far-fetched	soft-spoken
good-natured	stiff-necked
Latin-American	ten-foot
light-haired	un-American
long-needed	wild-eyed

2. Compound nouns.

Compound nouns consist of from two to as many as four parts. Practically every part of speech can become a component of a compound noun.

a. Two-part compound noun.
Coke is a *by-product* of coal. (preposition + noun)

b. Three-part compound noun.
My *brother-in-law* is a lawyer. (noun + preposition + noun)

c. Four-part compound noun.
Harry is a *jack-of-all-trades*. (noun + preposition + adjective + noun)

Other examples of compound nouns are the following:

court-martial	leveling-off
ex-president	looker-on
fellow-citizen	mother-in-law
forget-me-not	secretary-treasurer
go-between	son-in-law
great-grandson	tête-à-tête

3. Compound words with *half*, *quarter*, or *self* as the first element.

half-and-half	self-conceit
half-asleep	self-control
half-truth	self-interest
quarter-final	self-made
quarter-hour	self-respect
quarter-share	self-sacrifice

4. Compound words made from a single capital letter and a noun or participle:

A-flat	S-curve
F-sharp	T-shirt

5. "Improvised" compounds:

holier-than-thou	make-believe
know-it-all	never-say-die
long-to-be-remembered	never-to-be-forgotten

6. Compound numerals from twenty-one through ninety-nine:

thirty-three	sixty-seven
forty-six	eighty-five

7. The numerator and denominator of fractions:

four-fifths	three-quarters
one-half	two-thirds

If the hyphen already appears in either numerator or denominator it is omitted in writing the fraction:

twenty-one thirds   three ten-thousandths

GENERAL CAUTIONS IN USING THE HYPHEN

a. All the examples cited above were checked in a good desk dictionary. If your dictionary differs, don't hesitate to take its word.

b. Do not use a hyphen when two adjectives preceding a noun are independent:

She wore a *faded yellow* hat.

c. Do not use a hyphen when an adverb modifies an adjective:

She was a *highly trained* secretary.

d. Do not use a hyphen between double terms that denote a single office or rank:

Major General Jones   *Executive Director* Adams

e. Omit the hyphen in writing a fraction which is not an adjective:

He ate up *one half* of the pie.

f. Do not use a hyphen with reflexive pronouns:

herself   himself   yourselves

g. Many compounds formerly spelled separately or with a hyphen are now written as single words:

almighty   hateful   inasmuch   namesake

Once again, but finally, the only way to be sure about every compound word is to consult your dictionary.

Now apply what you have learned about compounds in the following exercise. In each of these phrases, decide whether the italicized expression should be written as one word, with hyphens, or as separate words. If you get stuck, consult your dictionary.

1. some *air minded* legislators
2. an important *air base*
3. excessive *rain fall*
4. a *base ball* game
5. in the *Far East*
6. a *battle hardened* veteran
7. the age of *twenty seven*
8. at *loose ends*
9. given a *rain check*
10. several *teen agers*

11. a *self satisfied* expression
12. a *holier than thou* attitude
13. in the *ante room*
14. a torn *book mark*
15. a broken *carpet sweeper*
16. in a *department store*
17. standing *flat footed*
18. got his *sheep skin*
19. *two way* road ahead
20. a sale of *re treads*
21. having only *self less* motives
22. a great *do it yourself* man
23. *un American* activities
24. an *anti climactic* ending
25. having been *re elected*
26. the *under developed* countries
27. a *well organized* conspiracy
28. a medieval *city state*
29. this *widely held* misconception
30. a sale of *pre empted* land
31. a row of *semi detached* houses
32. the fund was *over subscribed*
33. a *never to be forgotten* experience
34. an experience *never to be forgotten*
35. in the *living room*
36. a *pre dated* contract
37. a *poverty stricken* region
38. he was *well known* as an auctioneer
39. an attack of *home sickness*
40. a *hard hearted* landlord

10

USE A DICTIONARY: CAPITALIZATION

Strictly speaking, a discussion of capital letters does not belong in a spelling book. One can argue with some reason that if a word contains all the right letters in the right places it is correctly spelled.

It is true that man has had to invent distinctions between capital letters and small letters and that these distinctions have varied from century to century and from author to author. At one time, for example, it was customary to capitalize all nouns, as it still is in writing German. Gradually, however, certain modern customs involving capital letters evolved. These customs aren't particularly logical. Perhaps because capitalization is as illogical as spelling and quite as much a matter of accident and convention it deserves discussion in this book.

THE CONVENTIONS OF CAPITAL LETTERS

To misspell is to violate a convention; to use capital letters wrongly is to violate a convention. And breaking conventions, as all of us know, can cause us embarrassment, anguish, money, or all three. Many people firmly believe that mistakes in using capital and small letters are as serious as misspelling. Indeed, they feel that such mistakes *are* misspellings. Probably they are right.

The applications of capitalization are so numerous, and so loaded with exceptions, that firm rules and principles cannot apply to every possible example. A few underlying principles may be helpful and are given below. The only sound principle for you to follow is *use a dictionary.*

CAPITALIZING FIRST WORDS

1. Capitalize the first word of every sentence and the first word of every direct quotation.

   The engine needs repair.
   He asked, "Does the engine need repair?"

When only a part of a direct quotation is included within a sentence, it is usually not begun with a capital letter.

> The reporter told me that the official said he felt "fine" but thought that he should "take it easy" for a few weeks.

CAPITALIZING PROPER NOUNS

2. Capitalize proper nouns. Proper nouns include:

   a. Names of people and titles used for specific persons: George Washington, Theodore Roosevelt, the President, the Senator, the Treasurer, the General, Mr. Chairman, Father, Mother.

   b. Names of countries, states, regions, localities, other geographic areas, and the like: United States, England, Illinois, the Far East, the Dust Bowl, the Midwest, the Solid South, the Rocky Mountains, the Sahara Desert, the Connecticut River, Lake Michigan.

   c. Names of streets: Michigan Boulevard, Fifth Avenue, Ross Street, Old Mill Road.

   d. Names of the Deity and personal pronouns referring to Him: God, Heavenly Father, Son of God, Jesus Christ, Saviour, His, Him, Thy, Thine.

   e. Names for the Bible and other sacred writings: Bible, the Scriptures, Book of Genesis, Revelations, Koran.

   f. Names of religions and religious groups: Protestantism, Roman Catholicism, Presbyterian, Jesuit, Unitarian, Judaism, Shinto.

   g. Names of the days and the months (but *not* the seasons): Monday, Tuesday, etc.; January, February, etc.; summer, winter, autumn, fall, spring.

   h. Names of schools, colleges, universities: Woodberry Forest School, Kentucky Military Institute, Davidson College, Cornell University.

   i. Names of historic events, eras, and holidays: Revolutionary War, Christian Era, Middle Ages, Renaissance, the Fourth of July, Labor Day, Thanksgiving.

   j. Names of races, organizations, and members of each: Indian, Negro, Malay, League of Women Voters, the Junior League, American Academy of Science, National League, San Francisco Giants, Big Ten Conference, an Elk, a Shriner, a Socialist.

k. Vivid personifications: Fate, Star of Fortune, Destiny, the power of Nature, the paths of Glory, the chronicles of Time, Duty's call.

l. Trade names: Bon Ami, Mr. Clean, Ry-Krisp, Wheaties, Anacin.

Note: If the reference is to any one of a class of persons or things rather than to a specific person or thing, do not capitalize the noun or adjective:

> He is not a captain.
> His name is Captain Draper.
> I am going to a theater.
> He is at the Bijou Theater.
> He attended high school.
> He attended Sumter High School.
> In college he took history and biology.
> In college he took History 12 and Biology 3.

CAPITALS IN POETRY AND IN TITLES

3. Capitalize the first word of every line of poetry:

> I held it truth, with him who sings
> To one clear harp in divers tones,
> That men may rise on stepping-stones
> Of their dead selves to higher things.
> —TENNYSON

4. Capitalize each important word in the title of a book, play, magazine, musical composition, etc.:

> *The Decline and Fall of the Roman Empire*
> *You Can't Go Home Again*
> *Romeo and Juliet*
> *Atlantic Monthly*
> *Madame Butterfly*

THE CARELESS USE OF CAPITAL LETTERS

5. Avoid unnecessary and careless use of capitals.

a. Do not carelessly make small (lower-case) letters so large that they resemble capitals (upper-case letters).

b. Do not capitalize names of points of the compass unless they refer to a specific section.

> He lives in the West.
> He walked west along the street.

c. Capitalize nouns such as *father* and *mother* if they are not preceded by a possessive.

> Your father is a tall man.
> I love Father very much.
> My sister thinks I am noisy,
>   but Grandpa says I am not.

Apply what you have learned about capitalization to situations presented in the following sentences. For each number in parentheses, decide whether the following word should begin with a capital or small letter.

The reporters next asked (1) general Coole for his opinion. The (2) general's only response was a terse (3) "no comment."

(1) _____; (2) _____; (3) _____.

At the first glow of dawn in the (4) east, the calm of the (5) equatorial jungle is shattered by an astonishing racket of bird cries and monkey calls; (6) even a person used to it is momentarily stunned.

(4) _____; (5) _____; (6) _____.

"If the (7) president is to retain the (8) southern vote," said Anderson, (9) "he will have to sacrifice some inner-city support in the (10) north."

(7) _____; (8) _____; (9) _____; (10) _____.

During the committee hearings (11) chairman Topper made frequent use of apt quotations from the (12) bible, which were probably more familiar to his (13) baptist constituents in (14) southern Mississippi than to the public at large.

(11) _____; (12) _____; (13) _____; (14) _____.

"I knew I could count on (15) mother's support," she said, (16) "but how could I break the news to my (17) father? (18) he's dead set against my leaving home."

(15) _____; (16) _____; (17) _____; (18) _____.

In recent years it has been customary for the (19) national (20) league to win the (21) all-star (22) game but to lose the (23) world (24) series, yet nothing is likely to shake the confidence of that (25) league's fans in its superiority.

(19) _____; (20) _____; (21) _____; (22) _____; (23) _____;
(24) _____; (25) _____.

The rather chilling scientific name for the (26) grizzly (27) bear, once found throughout the (28) rocky (29) mountain (30) range, is *Ursus horribilis,* although it is in fact less dangerous than the (31) polar (32) bear, which carries the relatively mild designation of (33) *thalarctos* (34) *maritimus.*

(26) _____; (27) _____; (28) _____; (29) _____; (30) _____;
(31) _____; (32) _____; (33) _____; (34) _____.

One of the little-noticed features of (35) homecoming (36) day was an illustrated lecture by (37) professor Folkes on archaeological finds in the (38) middle (39) east, of interest to students of both (40) history and the (41) fine (42) arts.

(35) _____; (36) _____; (37) _____; (38) _____; (39) _____;
(40) _____; (41) _____; (42) _____.

Several characteristics of the repellent (43) utopia pictured in Aldous Huxley's novel *Brave* (44) *new World,* supposedly a projection into the twenty-fifth (45) century, are already appearing in today's (46) world.

(43) _____; (44) _____; (45) _____; (46) _____.

The teams of many (47) universities are known by their totem animals, such as the (48) badger, chosen by Wisconsin, and the (49) wolverine, by Michigan, but some other schools, such as Syracuse (50) university, maintain their athletic ferocity without the aid of feral symbols. In football games of recent years, perhaps by a decree of (51) nature, the (52) wolverines have usually overcome the (53) badgers.

(47) _____; (48) _____; (49) _____; (50) _____; (51) _____;
(52) _____; (53) _____.

LEARN A FEW SIMPLE RULES OF SPELLING

If you happen to study carefully a number of words which have similar characteristics you can make some generalizations about their spelling. In fact, observers have been doing just this for more than a century with the result that nearly fifty spelling rules have been formulated.

Generalizations about the groupings of letters which form classes of words will definitely help some people to spell more correctly. Those with good visual or motor memories will not need them. Other people apparently have a psychological block against rules. But experience has shown that rules—or at least a few of the more basic ones—do help some people to spell correctly certain classes of words. Applying spelling rules is only one approach to correct spelling; it may be more or less helpful to you than the other methods of attack presented in this book.

The rules which follow, with their corollaries, are simple and easily learned. Mastering them may help you to eliminate a large number of recurring errors in fairly common words. If this approach works for you, then consult other books on spelling or the section on orthography (spelling according to standard usage) in *Webster's New Collegiate Dictionary* for additional rules. The six rules stated and illustrated below are those which the author's experience has shown to be most useful and to apply to the largest number of commonly misspelled words.

Before studying the rules which follow, you should understand a few basic principles about them.

First, it is doubtful that anyone ever improved his spelling merely by saying a rule over and over to himself. Words come first, rules second; you should apply a rule, not merely memorize and mouth it.

Second, there are exceptions to every rule. And since there are so many exceptions you will need to use an additional approach:

improve your visual or motor memory; use some remembering trick; consult your dictionary.

Third, the corollary and the reverse of every spelling rule are as important as the rule itself. For example, in the first rule given below, you are shown when not to use *i* before *e,* but the reverse of this pattern is fully as important and must be kept in mind and applied. Learning only part of a rule is about as silly and timewasting as looking up a word in a dictionary and learning only one meaning of it, or only its spelling.

THE *EI-IE* RULE

One of the most frequent causes of misspelling is not knowing whether to write *ei* or *ie* in literally scores of everyday words. In fact, about one thousand fairly common words contain *ei* or *ie.* It helps to know that *ie* occurs in twice as many words as *ei,* but the problem is not thereby solved.

The basic rule may be stated in one of the best-known pieces of doggerel ever written:

> Write *i* before *e*
> Except after *c*
> Or when sounded like *a*
> As in *neighbor* and *weigh.*

This rule, or principle, applies only when the pronunciation of *ie* or *ei* is a long *e* (as in *he*) or the sound of the *a* in *fade.*

Here's another way to summarize the rule and its reverse:

> When the sound is long *e* (as in *piece*)
>   put *i* before *e* except after *c.*
> When the sound is not long *e* (as it is not in *weigh*)
>   put *e* before *i.*

Still another way to state this principle is this: When the *e* sound is long, *e* comes first after *c* but *i* comes first after all other consonants:

ceiling	deceit	receipt
conceit	deceitful	receive
conceited	deceive	
conceive	perceive	

achieve	apiece	believe
aggrieve	belief	besiege

bier	grieve	reprieve
brief	handkerchief	retrieve
cashier	hygiene	shield
chandelier	mischief	shriek
chief	piece	siege
field	pier	thief
fiend	pierce	wield
frontier	priest	wiener
grief	relieve	yield

This much of the rule is fairly simple: usually you write *ie*, except after the letter *c*, when you write *ei*—provided the sound is long *e*. The last two lines of the doggerel refer to words in which *ei* or *ie* sounds like *a*. Fortunately, only a few everyday words fall in this group, among them:

beige	heir	surveillance
chow mein	ncigh	vcil
deign	neighbor	vein
eight	reign	weigh
feint	rein	weight
freight	skein	
heinous	sleigh	

A few words are either exceptions to this basic *ei-ie* rule or are not fully covered by the four lines of doggerel. The best advice is to learn the following words by some method other than trying to apply the rule, which doesn't work here:

caffeine	height	seize
codeine	hierarchy	seizure
either	leisure	sheik
Fahrenheit	neither	sleight
fiery	protein	stein
financier	Reid (proper name)	weird

Summary

1. Use *ie* generally when sounded as long *e* (he).
2. Use *ei* after *c* when sounded as *e* (he).
3. Use *ei* when sounded as *a* (*eight*).
4. Watch out for exceptions.

THE FINAL Y RULE

Forming the plural of nouns ending in *y* has already been discussed on pages 81–83. But the rule applies also to words other than nouns and their plurals. The basic principle is this:

a. Words ending in *y* preceded by a consonant usually change *y* to *i* before any suffix except one beginning with *i*:

angry, angrily
beauty, beautiful
busy, busily, business
carry, carries, carrying
dignify, dignified, dignifying
easy, easier, easily
empty, emptier, emptiness
happy, happier, happiness
lovely, lovelier, loveliness
lucky, luckier, luckily
marry, married, marriage
merry, merrier, merrily, merriment
pity, pitiful, pitying
pretty, prettier, prettiness
study, studied, studious
try, tried, trying

b. Words ending in *y* preceded by a vowel do not change *y* to *i* before suffixes or other endings:

annoy, annoyed, annoyance   employ, employer
betray, betrayal   stay, stayed, staying

To the two parts of this "final *y*" rule there are so many exceptions that some experts feel the rule is not helpful. However, the exceptions among commonly used words are not numerous and can easily be mastered by some other approach suggested in this book. Here are some everyday words which follow neither part of the "final *y*" principle:

baby, babyhood   day, daily
busy, busyness (state of being lady, ladyship
  busy)   lay, laid

pay, paid   slay, slain
say, said   wry, wryly, wryness
shy, shyly, shyness

THE FINAL *E* RULE

Hundreds of everyday English words end in *e,* and hundreds and hundreds more consist of such words plus suffixes: *hope, hoping; come, coming; safe, safety,* etc. In our pronunciation nearly all *e*'s at the end of words are silent (not pronounced): *advice, give, live,* etc. Actually, the function of a final silent *e* is to make the vowel of the syllable long: *rate* but *rat; mete* but *met; bite* but *bit; note* but *not,* etc.

With those facts in mind we can now proceed to a rule which covers more words than any other spelling rule, many of them common words frequently misspelled. Here it is:

Final silent *e* is usually dropped before a suffix beginning with a vowel but is retained before a suffix beginning with a consonant.

advise, advising   hate, hateful
amuse, amusing, amusement   hope, hoping, hopeless
argue, arguing   ice, icy
arrive, arrival   judge, judging
awe, awesome   like, likable
bare, barely, bareness   live, livable
believe, believing, believable   love, lovable
bite, biting   move, movable, movement
care, careful, careless   owe, owing
come, coming   purchase, purchasing
desire, desirable   safe, safely, safety
dine, dining   sincere, sincerely
excite, exciting, excitement   sure, surely, surety
extreme, extremely   use, usable, useless

This basic rule is clear enough, but it does not cover all words ending in silent *e.* Here are some additions and exceptions to the general principle:

a. Silent *e* is retained when *ing* is added to certain words, largely to prevent them from being confused with other words:

dye, dyeing to contrast with *die, dying*

singe, singeing to contrast with *sing, singing*
swinge, swingeing to contrast with *swing, swinging*
tinge, tingeing to contrast with *ting, tinging*

b. Silent *e* is retained in still other words before a suffix beginning with a vowel. Sometimes this is done for the sake of pronunciation, sometimes for no logical reason at all:

acre, acreage	line, lineage
cage, cagey	mile, mileage
here, herein	shoe, shoeing
hoe, hoeing	there, therein

c. Silent *e* is dropped before a suffix beginning with a consonant in certain common words such as:

abridge, abridgment	nine, ninth
acknowledge,	nurse, nursling
acknowledgment	possible, possibly
argue, argument	probable, probably
awe, awful	true, truly
double, doubly	twelve, twelfth
due, duly	whole, wholly
incredible, incredibly	wise, wisdom
judge, judgment	

d. Silent *e* is retained in words ending in *ce* or *ge* even when suffixes beginning with vowels (*-able* and *-ous*) are added. This is done for the sake of pronunciation: to prevent giving a hard sound (*k* or hard *g*) to the *c* or *g:*

marriage, marriageable	advantage, advantageous
notice, noticeable	courage, courageous
service, serviceable	outrage, outrageous

e. A few words ending in *ie* in which the *e* is silent change *ie* to *y* before adding *ing*. Presumably this change occurs to prevent two *i*'s from coming together:

die, dying	tie, tying (or tieing)
lie, lying	vie, vying

THE INSERTED *K* RULE

The letter *k* is usually added to words ending in *c* before a suffix beginning with *e, i,* or *y.* This is done in order to prevent mispronunciation: note the different pronunciations, for example, of *picnicking* and *icing.* Only a few common words are involved in this rule, but they are frequently misspelled:

colic, colicky

frolic, frolicked, frolicking

mimic, mimicked,
  mimicking

panic, panicky

picnic, picnicked, picnicker

politic, politicking

shellac, shellacked,
  shellacking

traffic, trafficked, trafficking

This rule must be applied carefully. Note, for example, the words *frolicsome* and *mimicry.* Without adding a *k,* each *c* remains hard.

THE FINAL CONSONANT RULE

The rule for doubling final consonants is somewhat complicated, but mastering it and its parts will prevent many common misspellings. Despite its complexity, it is one of the most useful rules for spelling.

  a. Words of one syllable and those of more than one accented on the last syllable, when ending in a single consonant (except *x*) preceded by a single vowel, double the consonant before a suffix beginning with a vowel.

This rule is fairly detailed, but it will repay careful study. It is especially helpful in forming the past tense, past participle, and present participle of many frequently used verbs. It is also helpful in forming the comparative and superlative degrees of adjectives. Here is a list of only a few of the thousands of words to which this principle applies:

acquit, acquitted, acquitting, acquittal
admit, admitted, admitting, admittance
begin, beginning, beginner
clan, clannish
control, controlled, controller
drop, dropped, dropping

equip, equipped, equipping
forget, forgetting, forgettable, unforgettable
man, mannish
occur, occurred, occurring, occurrence
overlap, overlapped, overlapping
plan, planned, planning
prefer, preferred, preferring
red, redder, reddest, redden
refer, referred, referring
run, running, runner
swim, swimming, swimmer
tax, taxes
tin, tinny
transfer, transferred, transferring

b. If the accent is shifted to an earlier syllable when the ending is added, do not double the final consonant:

confer, conferring, but conference
defer, deferring, but deference
infer, inferring, but inference
prefer, preferring, but preference

c. Cautions and exceptions:

1) Derivatives from basic words that change pronunciation from a long to short vowel follow the doubling rule:

bite, biting, but bitten
inflame, inflamed, but inflammable
write, writing, but written

2) Words ending in a final consonant preceded by *two* vowels do not double the final consonant:

appear, appeared, appearing, appearance
need, needed, needing, needy
train, trained, training, trainee

3) Words ending in *two* consonants do not double the final consonant:

bend, bending (not bendding)

insist, insisted (not insistted)
turn, turned (not turnned)

4) Words not accented on the final syllable do not ordinarily double the final consonant:

benefit, benefited (but fit, fitted)
happen, happened, happening
murmur, murmured, murmuring

A helpful word in fixing this principle in your mind is *combat.* It may be pronounced with the accent on either syllable, but note the spelling:

combat′	combatted	combatting
com′bat	combated	combating

5) Like all spelling rules, this one for doubling has many exceptions or apparent exceptions. Rather than try to apply the rule slavishly you would gain by learning the following through some other approach suggested in this book:

cancellation	gaseous	overstepping
chagrined	handicapped	questionnaire
chancellor	humbugged	tranquillity
crystallize	legionnaire	transferable
excellence	metallurgy	transference
excellent	outfitter	zigzagged

THE "ONE PLUS ONE" RULE

When a prefix ends in the same letter with which the main part of the word begins, be sure that both letters are included.

When the main part of a word ends in the same letter with which a suffix begins, be sure that both letters are included.

When two words are combined, the first ending with the same letter with which the second begins, be sure that both letters are included.

Some spelling difficulties caused by prefixes and suffixes have been discussed in Chapter 6. The rule just stated in three parts is both supplementary and complementary to that discussion. It will take care of a larger number of often misspelled words such as:

accidentally	glowworm	really
bathhouse	illiterate	roommate
bookkeeping	interrelation	soulless
brownness	irresponsible	suddenness
cleanness	meanness	transshipment
coolly	misspelling	underrate
cruelly	occasionally	unnecessary
dissatisfied	overrated	unneeded
dissimilar	override	unnoticed
drunkenness	overrun	withholding

The only important exception to this rule is *eighteen* which, of course, is not spelled *eightteen*. Also, keep in mind that the same three consonants are never written solidly together: *cross-stitch*, not *crossstitch; still-life*, not *stilllife*. See the discussion of the hyphen (compound words) on pages 90–91.

12

SPELL CAREFULLY

This is a short chapter, but its brevity bears no relationship to its importance in spelling correctly. Actually, this chapter discusses the cause of at least half of the spelling mistakes made; for this reason it is probably the most important chapter in this book.

When writing, you concentrate on what you are trying to say and not on such matters as grammar, punctuation, and spelling. This concentration is both proper and understandable. But in your absorption you are quite likely to make errors of various sorts, including some in spelling, which result from haste or carelessness, not ignorance. When you discover a mistake of this kind, or it is pointed out to you, you may reply "Oh, I know better. I just wasn't watching," or "thinking" or "being careful" or whatever excuse you choose to make.

CARELESSNESS AND HASTE

Unfortunately, a mistake in spelling is a mistake until corrected. Your reader will not know, or care, what caused it. The office manager who received a letter from one of his staff recently inducted into the U.S. Army was delighted to hear from him but was more annoyed than puzzled to read: "It was the *frist* time we had to march ten miles and I nearly *collasped*." Certainly the young soldier knew better; he intended to write *first* and *collapsed* but, through haste, carelessness, or failure to proofread, the mistakes went through.

Isn't it fair to suggest that since so many English words really are difficult to spell, we should be careful with those we actually know? And yet it is the simple, easy words which nearly everyone *can* spell that cause over half the errors commonly made. Listed below are twenty words which the author has repeatedly found misspelled in letters, reports, and student papers. They are so easy that you are likely to look at them scornfully and say "I would never misspell any one of them." The fact is that you probably do misspell some of these words, on occasion, or other words just as simple:

all right, *not* alright	piano, *not* panio
a lot, *not* alot	radio, *not* raido
Britain, *not* Britian	religion, *not* regilion
curl, *not* crul	research, *not* reaserch
doesn't, *not* does'nt	surprise, *not* supprise
forty, *not* fourty	third, *not* thrid
high school, *not* highschool	thirty, *not* thrity
in fact, *not* infact	thoroughly, *not* throughly
in spite, *not* inspite	whether, *not* wheather
ninety, *not* ninty	wouldn't, *not* would'nt

Errors of this sort are easy to make. Our pen or pencil slips; a finger hits the wrong key; our minds wander. Even excellent spellers often repeatedly make such silly mistakes. What's the remedy?

PROOFREADING

Well, merely glancing over or even rereading what you've written is not likely to uncover all such errors. When we read we usually see only the outlines, or shells, of words. Only poor readers need to see individual letters as such; most of us comprehend words and even groups of words at a glance. As our eyes move along a line we neither see nor recognize individual letters and this, of course, is as it should be.

But have you ever noticed how much easier it is for you to detect spelling errors in someone else's writing than in your own? This may be due to the fact that we are looking for mistakes. Or it may be that we look more carefully at the writing of someone else than at our own because we are unfamiliar with it, are not previously aware of context, and have to pay closer attention in order to comprehend.

Whatever the reason for closer scrutiny, we narrow the range of our vision and thereby pick up mistakes hitherto unnoticed. In short, we detect careless errors in spelling not by reading but by *proofreading*.

It is indeed naïve for any of us to think that we can write rapidly without misspelling some words, even though we are good spellers. Only careful proofreading will uncover spelling errors in our own writing or, indeed, in anyone else's.

This kind of reading requires that we see words and phrases not as such but that we actually see every letter they contain. When each letter stands out distinctly, it is simple to detect errors in spelling.

VISION SPREAD

This triangle will show you how wide your vision (your sight spread) is. Look at the top of the triangle and then down. How far down can you go and still identify each letter in each line with a *single* glance? Your central vision is as wide as the line above the one where you cannot identify each letter *without moving your eyes at all:*

a

a r

a r d

a r d c

a r d c f

a r d c f g

a r d c f g x

a r d c f g x y

a r d c f g x y z

a r d c f g x y z p

a r d c f g x y z p w

People differ in their range of vision as they do in nearly everything else. But most people have difficulty in identifying more than six letters at a single glance. Some have a span of vision embracing only three or four letters. Whatever your span, you should not try to exceed it when you are carefully checking for spelling errors. If you do, you are reading—perhaps with excellent understanding— but you are not *proofreading.* And only proofreading will enable you to eliminate spelling errors due not to ignorance or stupidity but to carelessness.

Here is a list of forty frequently misspelled words. Some are spelled correctly here; some are not. In which of them can you identify each letter at a single glance? Which require you to move your eyes even if only slightly?

1. acquaint	3. all right	5. apear
2. against	4. amount	6. arise

7. around
8. basas
9. before
10. begining
11. careless
12. clothes
13. comming
14. considerable
15. decide
16. extremely
17. field
18. finishing
19. likelyhood
20. lonely
21. mere
22. noblity
23. noticeable
24. occupying
25. opportunity
26. optomistic
27. pamplet
28. perseverance
29. preferable
30. primative
31. process
32. pursue
33. recomendation
34. representative
35. restaurant
36. sandwitch
37. siege
38. twelfth
39. unmanageable
40. yield

Eleven of these words are misspelled. Did your proofreading catch them all? Check your findings: the following contain errors— 5, 8, 10, 13, 19, 22, 26, 27, 30, 33, 36.

Keep in mind that at least 50 percent of all errors come from omitting letters or transposing or adding them, writing two words as one or vice versa, and other similar acts of carelessness. Check and recheck, read and reread your writing until you have eliminated at least all the careless mistakes which everyone makes. There will still be errors enough of other kinds to keep you humble or angry.

Find out how well you can proofread. In the following paragraphs fifty words are misspelled. List these words on a sheet of paper by giving correct spellings of the errorful words. To help you get started, here are the incorrect spellings in the first paragraph: *registeration, recieve, writting, approximatly,* and *convient.* Keep proofreading until you locate exactly fifty words. If a word is spelled incorrectly more than once, list it only once.

1.

After I had been admitted to Atwood University and had completed my registeration, I was very much surprised to recieve a letter from my grandfather. Now, Grandfather was never very much of a man for writting letters, but approximatly every week or so his communications continued to arrive. I am sure that at times it was not convient for him to write (he as much as said so frequently), but he had the urge, so he said, to tell me of his own experiences at Atwood.

2.

Grandfather early wrote about my making friends. He had made the aquaintance, he said, of many people during his first weeks at Atwood, from whom he chose a few intimates. These people he had met in the classroom, at some of the fraternities, in the Union, in resturants, and on the atheletic field. He treated every one in a courtious manner and never cracked jokes at their expense; so doing, he had learned, was a sure way to forfiet their respect.

3.

One of Grandfather's closest associates was Bill Jones, whom he had met at one of the dormatories. Bill was a very tempermental person, but he had a genius for getting along with people, and Grandfather benefited greatly from his comradship. About the middle of the first semester they became roomates.

4.

From Bill Jones Grandfather learned much about the art of studying. Up to the time of their rooming togeather, Grandfather was much dissatisfied with his scholastic record, and even though he tried to learn to study, he sometimes was so poorly prepared, usually in mathmatics and English, that he was almost too embarassed to go to class. Bill made a begining of his work on Grandfather's scholarship by giving him simple explainations of his more difficult assignments, but he was more interested in teaching the methods and dicipline of study. Once Grandfather had mastered these, the maintainance of better marks became an easy task.

5.

One of Bill's secrets was concentration; if you divide your attention, you get nowhere. Another was not postponing getting to work. Grandfather admitted, for example, that the night before one test, he spent the evening playing pool at the Union. He had alloted two hours for his review, but the evening just seemed to dissappear, and when Grandfather got to his room, he was too tired to worry about his lack of knowlege, and went immediatly to bed. He was not much mistified when he failed the test, and he even thought of quiting school. But about that time he met Bill and aquired valuble study habits. No longer was he an irresponsable student, handicaped by a lack of study method. Study was now his first neccessary task. When the next test came, he was so good that he could spot an independant clause a paragraph away; and by the time of the punctuation test, he had mastered the comma, had good control of the semicoln, and was even using recklessly but correctly quite a number of appostrophes.

6.

In high school Grandfather had been a notorously poor speller. The adolescent love notes that Grandfather wrote to the girl accross the aisle contained so many wrongly spelled words that the young lady broke off the correspondance. Love couldn't erradicate Grandfather's spelling disease, and after this disasterous adventure he swore that he would overcome his trouble; but he didn't. It was method, not love, that Grandfather needed, and Bill Jones supplied the answer. Grandfather still spelled a word wrong occassionally, but he became so persistent in his study of the words spelled by rule, the tricky words, and the words spelled according to sylable that when he took the spelling test for the first time, he had only one mispelled word.

7.

I could go on and on telling of the refferences to college life made in Grandfather's letters, and of the many occurences of which he wrote. But I don't want to be accused of wordyness, and, anyway, I've given you a general idea of the content of these letters.

8.

Long before the end of the year I became conscious of the fact that Grandfather was trying to decieve me in a polite way; he was really giving me advice by means of his letters, but whenever I accused him of this fact, he swore to his innocense and vowed that his only object was to entertain me and, perhaps, keep me from becoming homesick. I never did quite beleive him.

13

USE MEMORY DEVICES

Suppose that someone suddenly asks you, "How many days in March?" You may be able to answer instantly, but if you are like most of us you will come up with the answer, "thirty-one," only after you have run through your head the familiar lines beginning, "Thirty days hath September ..." If so, what you have done is to use a device to aid memory.

One special kind of memory device has the rather imposing name of *mnemonics*. The word is pronounced *nee*-MON-*iks* and comes from a Greek word meaning "to remember." (Mnemosyne was the goddess of memory in Grecian mythology.) A mnemonic is a special aid to memory, a memory trick based on what psychologists refer to as "association of ideas," remembering something by associating it with something else. You may have been using mnemonics most of your life. The term applies to a very basic characteristic of the human mind.

For example, the author's physician used to confuse his home, office, and hospital telephone numbers. He could remember the exchanges all right, but frequently mixed up the three sets of four numbers which followed, sometimes with unfortunate results. Now he has no difficulty: his home number he associates with eating and the numbers 1-8-4-7 leap to mind as part of "Rogers 1847 Silverware." His office number represents the place where he *battles* the daily grind and he thinks of the date of the Battle of Hastings, "1066." The hospital is a place where many find peace and relief from pain; the doctor associates this idea with "1945," the end of World War II. His set of mnemonics has licked the problem for him. When the telephone company assigns different numbers he will probably invent other memory aids. In our own lives each of us quite likely uses many similar associations of ideas, however different they may be in details from those of the physician just mentioned.

MNEMONICS AS A SPELLING AID

Mnemonics *can* be used to improve spelling. The system will help some more than others and may not help some people at all. The entire system of association of ideas has been criticized because, of course, you can place a greater burden on your mind with elaborate mnemonics than is involved in the original item to be remembered. In addition, a memory aid that works for you may be useless to me, and vice versa. But a set of mental associations has proved useful to some people for spelling certain words, and a system of mnemonics is one legitimate approach to better spelling. The system is the main trade trick of memory experts for whom it works with astounding results.

As other chapters in this book try to show, the spelling of most words can be learned by improving visual or motor images and by spelling rules. But for each of us there probably is a small number of words the spelling of which is always troublesome. They fit no pattern; their spelling makes little or no sense. Learning them is a matter of sheer memory. For such words, an association of ideas may help. At least it will be more profitable than mouthing the hard words repeatedly or writing them over and over until they seem formless or grotesque.

Any mnemonic is a sort of crutch, something we use until we can automatically spell a given word without even thinking. But so is a rule a crutch, and, in a different sense, a dictionary is, too. In time, we can throw away our spelling crutches except on rare occasions; until then we can use them to avoid staggering and falling.

A mnemonic will be most helpful when you contrive it from some happening, or base it upon some person, meaningful in your life. That is, you must invent, or use, only mnemonics that have a *personal* association of ideas. Some of the mnemonics suggested below will help you; others will seem meaningless or downright silly. Some words which trouble you will not even be covered. You can then try devising mnemonics of your own for your particular spelling demons.

As was suggested in Chapter 5, a clue about the etymology or origin of a word will sometimes provide a mnemonic. Sometimes exaggerated pronunciation will form the association, the bond of relationship between word and spelling. Occasionally, breaking the word into parts will help. Sometimes a play on words will give a useful memory device. As you read the mnemonics below, you will note these and various other methods used in manufacturing them. On occasion, you will see that more than one method is used to phrase a mnemonic for the same word. Adapt for your use the most helpful one.

MEMORY CLUES TO SELECTED
TROUBLESOME WORDS

If none of these mnemonics proves helpful, you will at least have suggestions for "rolling your own." If another approach to correct spelling better suits your learning abilities, then skip what follows. At any rate, these memory clues have helped some people to spell correctly the words listed:

all right—Two words. Associate with **all correct** or **all wrong.**

anoint—Use **an oil** to **anoint** him (each **n** appears alone).

argument—I lost an **e** in that **argument.**

balloon—Remember the **ball** in **balloon.**

battalion—This comes from **battle;** it has the same double **t** and single **l.**

believe—You can't bel**ie**ve a **lie.**

business—Business is no **sin.**

calendar—The **D.A.R.** will meet soon.

capitol—A capit**o**l has a d**o**me (associate **o**).

cemetery—1. There is **ease** (**e**'s) in the cemetery.

   2. A place we get to with **ease** (**e**'s).

compliment—A compliment is what **I** like to get.

conscience—con + science.

corps—Don't kill a live body of men with an **e** (corpse).

definite—Definite comes from **finite.**

dependable—An **able** worker is depend**able.**

descendant—A descend**ant** has an **ancestor.**

desert—The Sahara (one **s**).

dessert—Strawberry **s**undae (two **s**'s).

dilemma—In a dil**emma** was **Emma.**

disappoint—dis + appoint.

dormitory—The French word for sleep is **dormir**.

ecstasy—There is no **x** in **ecstasy**.

embarrassed—1. Double **r**, double **s**, double trouble.
                2. **R**obert and **R**ose were shop stewards.

February—February makes one say "Br!"

genealogy—**Al** is interested in gene**al**ogy.

grammar—1. Accent the trouble spot: gramm**ar**.
          2. Don't **mar** your writing with bad gram**mar**.
          3. Write **g—r—a—m**: then start back: **m—a—r**.

hear—I **hear** with my **ear**.

indispensable—1. **Able** people are indispens**able**.
              2. This word refers to a thing one is not **able** to **dispense** with.
              3. **Sable** is indispen**sable** to some women.

infinite—Infinite comes from **finite**.

inoculate—Inoculate means to **in**ject.

irresistible—1. I am irresistible to the opposite sex.
          2. Lipstick is irresistible.

laboratory—People **labor** in a **labor**atory.

literature—It was an **era** of good lit**era**ture.

medicine—Associated with **medicinal**.

occasion—1. An occasion occurs.
          2. Don't be an **ass** on this occasion (one **s**).

occurrence—An occurrence may be a current event.

outrageous—The outrageous idea put me in a **rage**.

parallel—**All** lines are parallel.

piece—Have a **piece** of **pie**.

potatoes—Potatoes have eyes and **toes**.

preparation—1. From the base word prepare.
          2. This comes from *prae* + *parare* (to make ready).

principal—A principal rule is a **main** rule.

principle—A princip**le** is just a **rule**.

privilege—Some special privi**le**ges are **vile**.

professor—The abbreviation is **prof** (one **f**).

pronunciation—The **nun** knew pron**un**ciation.

pursuit—A pickpocket took my **purse**.

recommend—re + commend.

relative—Relative comes from **relate**.

repetition—Associate with "repeat."

resistance—Increase resis**tan**ce with **tan.**
ridiculous—Associate with **ridicule.**
seize—Seize him by the ear (**e** before **i**).
separate—1. Separate means "**a**part."
　　　　　　2. Accent the trouble spot: separate.
　　　　　　3. There is a **rat** in sepa**rat**e.
sergeant—Think of **serge + ant.**
siege—An army **si**ts before a city (**i** before **e**).
significant—"**Sign** if I cant" (can't).
stationary—This word means "st**a**nding."
stationery—This is used for writing l**e**tt**e**rs.
superintendent—A superintend**ent** collects **rent.**
supersede—1. Both first and last syllables begin with **s.**
　　　　　　　2. The word comes from Latin *sedeo*, "to sit."
surprise—That was **sur**ely a **sur**prise.
temperature—She lost her **temper at** the heat.
together—to + get + her.
tragedy—1. Every **age** has its tr**age**dy.
　　　　　　2. Old **age** may be a tr**age**dy.
tranquillity—Associate with **quill** (pens used in olden days).
vaccine—Vaccine is measured in **c**ubi**c c**entimeters (**cc's**).
villain—The **villa**in likes his **villa in** the country.
Wednesday—This word means "**Wed**en's day."

14

LISTING MISSPELLED WORDS

This chapter, the one with which many books on spelling begin, discusses an important phase of spelling study. It has been placed later for several reasons.

One reason is that learning to spell is an individual, highly personal matter. As we have discovered, a single approach to correct spelling will work for one person and not for another. Also, the words whose spelling gives you trouble may not be the words which bother me or any of your friends and acquaintances. Perhaps it would be more precise to say that, although certain words cause trouble for a majority of people, any list of commonly misspelled words will contain some that give you no difficulty and omit others that do. The very best list of words for you to study is the one you prepare yourself to meet your own needs and shortcomings.

THE VALUE OF SPELLING LISTS

There's a lot of waste in any spelling list, including the list of 860 words which follows. It is simple to prepare a list of "spelling demons" and assert that these are the "most frequently misspelled" words in the language. In a sense, this statement would be correct, but it fails to recognize that, although these words are likely to be misspelled when used, they aren't used very often. Learning to spell a long list of difficult words is about as silly as trying to swallow a dictionary or an encyclopedia. You use a dictionary when you need to tap its resources, just as you turn a faucet to get water from a reservoir. You consult a list of misspelled words only when you have a definite need.

Another reason for deferring this chapter to the end is that by now you should have a sound basis for considering its contents. It doesn't help to try to memorize a list of miscellaneous words. But with what you have learned about various attacks on the spelling problem you can now *study* words in a list and *apply* to them principles you have learned.

Furthermore, you will be able to ignore words which you can already spell "without thinking" and will be alert to add words which give you trouble but which don't appear.

Once again, this chapter should serve primarily to start you on a list of your personal spelling demons. These words will be ones you need to learn to spell because you use them. And they may be simple or difficult; short or long; everyday words or ones which, although rare to others, are a part of your working vocabulary. The only sound basis for any list of misspelled words is its *use* value.

Regardless of whether we are housewives, businessmen, clerks, truckdrivers, or physicians, we all use certain basic words many scores of times more often than any others in the language. Any spelling list should start with them, but, fortunately, they are never (or hardly ever) misspelled by anyone who can write at all. The most frequently used words in the English language are *and, the, to, you, your, in, for, of, we, is, I,* and *its.* These give no trouble except for some occasional confusion between *your* and *you're* and *its* and *it's.*

Once past this basic list, however, selecting frequently used words becomes more difficult. *Table* is an everyday word, but a baker might use *bread* and a physician might use *temperature* more often. It is reassuring to know, however, that it is neither the most simple and common words nor the ones primarily used in a trade, profession, or industry that provide major spelling difficulty. The words in between are the troublemakers. And here we do have some authoritative studies of frequency word use and frequency misspellings. The short list which follows is based upon one of these major studies.

THE TWENTY MOST OFTEN
MISSPELLED WORDS

Of the five hundred words occurring most frequently in our speech and writing only twenty ever cause anyone except very poor spellers any trouble whatever. Probably few, if any, of them bother you. Here is the list:

across	believe	business	don't
almost	brought	dollar	friend

government	quite	supply	through
laugh	receive	suppose	whether
possible	should	their	your

Keep in mind that these twenty words, along with 480 even more easily spelled ones, are certain to appear in your speech and writing many times as often as all other words in the language. The best approach of all to correct spelling is to *master* the simple, everyday words that you use over and over. Doing so will solve the greater part of your spelling problem.

According to another authoritative estimate, previously quoted, a basic list of only one thousand words appears in 90 percent of all writing. All of the thousand which involve spelling problems are included in the long list which follows. About 75 percent of the words which follow are among the words most often misspelled regardless of frequency use. The other 25 percent consist of words which the author has found repeatedly misspelled in business offices, in manuscripts submitted for magazine or book publication, and in college classrooms.

As suggested, many of the words you will have already mastered; you must supplement the list in accordance with your own needs. But remember to go slowly. Don't try to memorize the list. Thoroughly mastering five words a day is more productive than superficially learning one hundred.

And as you start studying the list of words, apply one or more of the varied approaches suggested in previous chapters. Examining these words without following one or several of the planned attacks discussed in this book will merely waste your time and result in further and prolonged frustration.

Consult your dictionary frequently. You must know the meaning of each of the words you are studying; otherwise, in your own writing you may correctly spell a perfectly good word but one which does not have the meaning you intended. Also, to keep this list within reasonable limits, not all forms of every word are shown; therefore, use your dictionary or one of the other approaches developed in previous chapters as a guide to word-building.

LIST OF 860 WORDS OFTEN MISSPELLED*

1. absence
2. absolutely
3. academic
4. accept
5. access

6. accessible
7. accident (accidentally)
8. accommodate (accommodations)
9. accompanying
10. accomplishment

11. according
12. accumulation
13. accurate
14. accuse
15. accustomed

16. ache
17. achievement
18. acknowledge (acknowledgment)
19. acquaint (acquaintance)
20. across

21. activities
22. actual (actually)
23. address
24. adequate
25. adjacent

26. admiration
27. adolescent
28. advantage
29. advantageous
30. advertisement

* The list given has been checked against some of the major studies of frequency word use and frequency misspelling of the last forty years, as follows:

William Niclaus Andersen, "Determination of a Spelling Vocabulary Based upon Written Correspondence," *University of Iowa Studies in Education*, II, No. 1 (1917).

Alfred Farrell, "Spelling as a College Subject," *Journal of Education*, CXXII (January, 1939), 20, 21.

Arthur I. Gates, *Spelling Difficulties in 3876 Words* (New York: Bureau of Publications, Teachers College, Columbia University, 1937).

John G. Gilmartin, *Gilmartin's Word Study*, rev. ed. (New York: Prentice-Hall, 1936).

Harry V. Masters, "A Study of Spelling Errors," *University of Iowa Studies in Education*, IV, No. 4 (1927–1929).

Thomas Clark Pollock, "Spelling Report," *College English*, XVI (November, 1954), 102–109.

Edward L. Thorndike and Irving Lorge, *The Teacher's Word Book of 30,000 Words* (New York: Bureau of Publications, Teachers College, Columbia University, 1944).

31. advice
32. advisable
33. advise
34. adviser
35. affect

36. afraid
37. aggravate
38. aggressive
39. aisle
40. allot (allotting)

41. allotment
42. allowance
43. all right
44. almost
45. alphabet

46. already
47. altar
48. alter
49. although
50. all together

51. altogether
52. amateur
53. ambitious
54. American
55. among

56. amount
57. analysis
58. analyze
59. announcement
60. annual

61. answer
62. antecedent
63. anticipation
64. antidote
65. antiseptic

66. anxiety
67. apartment
68. apology
69. apparatus
70. apparently

71. appearance
72. appendicitis
73. applied
74. appointment
75. appreciation

76. approach
77. appropriate
78. approval
79. approximately
80. arctic

81. argue (arguing)
82. argument
83. aroused
84. arrangement
85. article

86. ascend
87. assistance
88. association
89. athletic
90. attack

91. attendance
92. attitude
93. attractiveness
94. audience
95. author

96. authority
97. autobiography
98. autumn
99. auxiliary
100. available

101. awkward
102. bachelor
103. balloon
104. bargain
105. basically

106. basis
107. beautiful
108. beauty
109. becoming
110. beggar

111. beginning
112. behavior
113. believing
114. beneficial
115. benefit (benefited)

116. boundary
117. breath
118. breathe
119. Britain
120. business

121. cafeteria
122. calendar
123. campaign
124. candidate
125. capital

126. career
127. careless
128. carrying
129. category
130. celebrate

131. cemetery
132. century
133. certain
134. challenge
135. changeable

136. characteristic
137. chauffeur
138. cheerfulness
139. chiefly
140. chocolate

141. choose
142. chose
143. chosen
144. circumstance
145. clothes

146. coincidence
147. column
148. comfortably
149. commercial
150. commission

151. committee
152. communication
153. community
154. companies
155. comparatively

156. comparison
157. compatible
158. compel (compelled)
159. competence
160. competition

161. completely
162. complexion
163. compliment
164. composition
165. comprehension

166. concede
167. conceivable
168. conceive
169. concentrated
170. concern

171. condemn
172. confidence
173. congratulations
174. connoisseur
175. conscience

176. conscientious
177. conscious
178. consensus
179. consequently
180. considerable

181. consistent
182. consolation
183. contemporary
184. contempt (contemptuous)
185. continually

186. continuous
187. contribution
188. controlled
189. controversy
190. convenience

191. correspondence
192. councilor
193. counselor
194. countries
195. courageous

196. courtesy
197. criticism
198. criticize
199. cruel
200. curiosity

201. curriculum
202. customary
203. customer
204. cylinder
205. dangerous

206. dealt
207. deceive
208. decidedly
209. decision
210. defenseless

211. deficiency
212. deficient
213. definite (definitely)
214. definition
215. delinquent

216. democracy
217. demonstrated
218. dependent
219. depression
220. descendant

221. descent
222. describe (description)
223. desert
224. despair
225. desperate

226. desperation
227. dessert
228. destruction
229. determination
230. detriment

231. devices
232. difference
233. difficulty
234. dilemma
235. diminish

236. dining room
237. diphtheria
238. disappear
239. disappoint
240. disastrous

241. disciple
242. discipline
243. discoveries
244. discrimination
245. discuss

246. disease
247. dissatisfied
248. dissipate
249. distinguished
250. divide

251. divine
252. doctor
253. doesn't
254. dominant
255. dormitories

256. drunkenness
257. ecstasy
258. edition
259. education
260. effect

261. efficiency
262. efficient
263. eighth
264. eighty
265. either

266. elementary
267. eligible
268. eliminate
269. eloquently
270. embarrass

271. emergency
272. emigrate
273. eminent
274. emperor
275. emphasize

276. emptiness
277. encouragement
278. enemies
279. English
280. enormous

281. enough
282. enterprise
283. entertainment
284. enthusiasm
285. entirely

286. entrance
287. environment
288. equally
289. equipment
290. equipped

291. equivalent
292. escape
293. especially
294. essential
295. eventually

296. everybody
297. evidently
298. exaggerating
299. exceed
300. excellent

301. except
302. exceptionally
303. excess
304. excitable
305. exercise

306. exhausted
307. exhibit
308. exhilarate
309. existence
310. expectation

311. expenses
312. experience
313. experiment
314. explanation
315. extravagant

316. facilities
317. faithfulness
318. fallacy
319. familiar
320. families

321. fantasy
322. fascinating
323. favorite
324. feasible
325. February

326. fictitious
327. finally
328. financially
329. financier
330. foreign

331. foreword
332. formally
333. formerly
334. forty
335. forward

336. foundation
337. fourteen
338. fourth
339. fraternity
340. friendliness

341. fulfill
342. fundamental
343. funeral
344. furniture
345. further

346. gaiety
347. gauge
348. genius
349. gentleman
350. genuine

351. glorious
352. goggles
353. gorgeous
354. government
355. governor

356. grammar
357. grandeur
358. grievous
359. guarantee
360. guidance

361. handicapped
362. handkerchief
363. happening
364. happiness
365. harass

366. haughtiness
367. healthy
368. hear
369. heartily
370. heavier

371. height
372. helpful
373. here
374. heroes
375. heroines

376. hindrance
377. hopelessness
378. hoping
379. hospitality
380. huge

381. humiliate
382. humorous
383. hungry
384. hurriedly
385. hygiene

386. hypocrisy
387. hypocrite
388. ignorance
389. imaginary
390. imagine

391. immediately
392. immense
393. immigrant
394. impassable
395. important

396. impossible
397. inadequate
398. inauguration
399. incidentally
400. increase

401. incredible
402. indefinitely
403. independent
404. indictment
405. indispensable

406. individual
407. industrial
408. influence
409. influential
410. ingenious

411. initiative
412. innocence
413. insistence
414. installation
415. instructor

416. instrument
417. intellectual
418. intelligent
419. interest (interesting)
420. interference

421. interpretation
422. interruption
423. intolerance
424. introductory
425. invariable

426. involved
427. irrelevant
428. irresistible
429. irritable
430. island

431. its
432. it's
433. January
434. jealousy
435. jewelry

436. kindergarten
437. knowledge
438. labeled
439. laboratory
440. laboriously

441. language
442. leisurely
443. lengthening
444. libraries
445. license

446. lieutenant
447. lightening
448. lightning
449. likelihood
450. literature

451. liveliest
452. livelihood
453. liveliness
454. loneliness
455. lose (losing)

456. lovable
457. loyalty
458. luxuries
459. magazine
460. magnificent

461. maintenance
462. management
463. managing
464. maneuver
465. manufacturing

466. marriage
467. marriageable
468. material
469. mathematics
470. meanness

471. meant
472. mechanics
473. medicine
474. mentality
475. merchandise

476. metropolitan
477. millionaire
478. miniature
479. miscellaneous
480. mischief

481. mischievous
482. misspelled
483. modified
484. monotonous
485. month

486. moral
487. morale
488. mosquitoes
489. multiplication
490. muscle

491. musician
492. mysterious
493. narrative
494. nationalities
495. naturally

496. necessary
497. negative
498. Negro
499. Negroes
500. neighbor

501. neither
502. Niagara
503. niece
504. nineteen
505. ninety

506. ninth
507. noticeable
508. noticing
509. numerous
510. obstacle

511. occasion (occasionally)
512. occupying
513. occur (occurred)
514. occurrence
515. occurring

516. o'clock
517. omission
518. omit
519. omitted
520. operate

521. operation
522. opinion
523. opponent
524. opportunities
525. oppose

526. optimism
527. optimistic
528. organization
529. origin
530. originally

531. overwhelming
532. paid
533. pamphlet
534. pandemonium
535. pantomime

536. parallel
537. paralyze
538. participated
539. particularly
540. partner

541. passed
542. past
543. pastime
544. peace
545. peaceable

546. peculiarities
547. penniless
548. perceive
549. performance
550. permanent

551. permissible
552. permit
553. perseverance
554. persistent
555. personal

556. personnel
557. perspiration
558. persuade
559. pertain
560. phase

561. phenomenon
562. Philippines
563. philosophy
564. physical
565. physician

566. picnicking
567. piece
568. planned
569. planning
570. plausible

571. playwright
572. pleasant
573. politician
574. portrayed
575. possessions

576. possibility
577. possible
578. poverty
579. practically
580. prairie

581. precedent
582. preceding
583. predominant
584. prefer
585. preferable

586. preference
587. preferred
588. prejudice
589. preparation
590. prepare

591. prescription
592. presence
593. prevalence
594. previous
595. primitive

596. principal
597. principle
598. privilege
599. probably
600. procedure

601. proceed
602. process
603. professor
604. prominent
605. pronounce

606. pronunciation
607. propaganda
608. proprietor
609. provisions
610. psychology

611. punctuation
612. pursue
613. qualities
614. quantity
615. quarter

616. questionnaire
617. quiet
618. realize
619. really
620. receipt

621. receivable
622. receive
623. recognition
624. recognize
625. recollection

626. recommend
     (recommendation)
627. reference
628. referred
629. refrigerator
630. regard

631. regrettable
632. relative
633. relevant
634. relieve
635. religion

636. religious
637. remember
638. remembrance
639. reminisce
640. renowned

641. repentance
642. repetition
643. representative
644. requirements
645. research

646. resources
647. response
648. responsibility
649. restaurant
650. reverend

651. reverent
652. reviewing
653. rhythm
654. ridicule
655. ridiculous

656. righteous
657. rivalry
658. roommate
659. sacrifice
660. safety

661. sandwich
662. satirical
663. satisfaction
664. satisfied
665. Saturday

666. saucer
667. sausage
668. scarcity
669. scene
670. scenery

671. schedule
672. scheme
673. scholarship
674. scientific
675. secretary

676. seize
677. selection
678. semester
679. sentence
680. separate

681. seriousness
682. several
683. severely
684. shepherd
685. shining

686. shoulder
687. shriek
688. siege
689. significance
690. similar

691. sincerely
692. situation
693. solution
694. sophomore
695. sorrowful

696. source
697. sovereignty
698. specialization
699. specifically
700. specimen

701. spectacle
702. speech
703. sponsor
704. statement
705. stationary

706. stationery
707. stenographer
708. stopping
709. straighten
710. strength

711. strenuous
712. stubborn
713. studied
714. studying
715. subscription

716. substantiate
717. substitute
718. subtle
719. succeeding
720. successful

721. suddenness
722. sufficient
723. summarize
724. summary
725. superintendent

726. supersede
727. superstitious
728. supervisor
729. suppose
730. suppress

731. surprise
732. surrounded
733. susceptible
734. suspense
735. suspicious

736. swimming
737. syllable
738. symbol
739. symmetrical
740. synonymous

741. system
742. tactfulness
743. technical
744. technique
745. temperament

746. temperate
747. temperature
748. temporarily
749. tenant
750. tendency

751. tenement
752. territory
753. than
754. their
755. then

756. theories
757. therefore
758. they're
759. thirtieth
760. thirty

761. thoroughly
762. thought
763. thousand
764. to
765. together

766. tomorrow
767. too
768. tradition
769. tragedy
770. transferred

771. transportation
772. tremendous
773. trespass
774. truly
775. try (tried)

776. Tuesday
777. twelfth
778. twentieth
779. two
780. typical

781. tyranny
782. unanimous
783. unbelievable
784. uncivilized
785. unconscious

786. uncontrollable
787. undesirable
788. undoubtedly
789. uneasiness
790. unforgettable

791. universities
792. unmanageable
793. unnecessary
794. until
795. unusual

796. usage
797. useful
798. usual
799. usually
800. vacuum

801. valleys	831. weird
802. valuable	832. whenever
803. varieties	833. where
804. various	834. wherever
805. vaudeville	835. whether
806. vegetable	836. whole
807. vengeance	837. wholesale
808. ventilate	838. wholly
809. verbatim	839. whose
810. vernacular	840. wintry
811. versatile	841. withal
812. veteran	842. withholding
813. vicinity	843. witnessed
814. victim	844. wonder
815. view	845. wonderful
816. village	846. wrench
817. villain	847. writing
818. villainous	848. written
819. vinegar	849. yacht
820. virtuous	850. Yankee
821. visible	851. Yiddish
822. vitamin	852. yield
823. volume	853. your
824. waive	854. you're
825. wander	855. yourself
826. warranted	856. zealot
827. wave	857. zenith
828. wealthiest	858. zero
829. weather	859. zigzag
830. Wednesday	860. zinc

Quite likely, this list of 860 words does not contain a few that give you most trouble. Now would be an excellent time to start your own list of "spelling demons."

15

TWENTY-FIVE
TROUBLESOME BEGINNINGS
AND ENDINGS

The preceding fourteen chapters of this little book have treated every
major and minor approach to better spelling that has ever been sen-
sibly attempted. There remain, however, a few trouble spots that
cannot neatly be tucked into any of the earlier chapters. Several of
the comments and recommendations that follow have been briefly
touched on but deserve fuller treatment.

1. ac-, acc-.
Numerous everyday words begin with *ac-*:

ace	acid	acne
ache	academic	acquire
acrid	action	active

acc- is the correct spelling when what follows is *l, o, r,* or *u:*

acclimate	accomplish	accrue
accuse	accompany	account
accustom	accredit	

Note these exceptions: *acorn, across, acute.* Words like *accident*
and *accede* cause no trouble because each *c* is separately pronounced.

2. -acious, -aceous, -atious.
These troublesome endings are pronounced the same, but by
far the most common spelling is *-acious:*

gracious	audacious	pugnacious

When in doubt, use *-acious.* Only a few words end in *-aceous*
and *-atious:*

curvaceous	herbaceous	sebaceous
vexatious	flirtatious	ostentatious

3. af-, aff-.

When *a* is the prefix of a word beginning with *f, af-* is, of course, the correct usage:

afield	afire	afresh
afloat	aflutter	afoot

Also beginning with -af are such words as *Africa* and *afraid*. Before a vowel or the consonants *l* and *r, aff-* is the accepted spelling:

affable	affect	affidavit
afford	affront	affluent

4. ag-, agg-.

When it is a prefix to a full word, *ag-* is the standard spelling:

aglow	aglitter	agleam

Ag- is also correct when it precedes *r* in certain words:

aground	agree	agrarian
agriculture	agronomy	agreement

The following words begin with *agg-*:

aggressive	aggregate	agglomerate
aggravate	aggrandize	aggrieved

5. al-, all-.

Visual memory is about your only help in spelling words with these beginnings. The following common words begin with *all-*:

allergy	allowance	allege
alloy	alligator	alleviate
allot	ally	allocate

Words beginning with *al-* are quite numerous:

almanac	aloft	aloof
almost	aloe	altogether
almighty	alone	aloft
alimony	along	alphabet

6. ap-, app-.

Don't omit the second *p* in words like these:

apply	appoint	apparent
appear	approach	apparel
apparatus	approve	appeal
approximate	application	appetite

Ap- words are even more numerous than those beginning with *app-*:

apartment	apart	aphorism
apology	apathy	apiece
apostrophe	ape	aplomb
aperture	apex	apoplexy
apostate	apostle	apothecary

7. -ard, -ards.

In words like *backward* and *upward*, the ending without *s* (*-ard*) is the adjective form (a *backward* step, an *upward* movement). As an adverb, such a word may be spelled with or without an *s*; walking *backward* or *backwards*. The following words are all spelled correctly:

downward, downwards	toward, towards
forward, forwards	homeward, homewards

Recommendation: Use the spelling without *s* wherever possible since it is shorter.

8. -ayed, -aid.

Some verbs ending in *-ay* form their past tense by adding *-ed:*

play, played	betray, betrayed	pray, prayed

But the past tenses of most verbs ending in *-ay* are formed with *-aid:*

pay, paid	outlay, outlaid	say, said
lay, laid	mislay, mislaid	waylay, waylaid

9. col-, coll-.

Before any vowel, *coll-* is more frequently correct than *col-*:

collar	collect	collide
collapse	college	collaborate
collie	collusion	collier
colloquy	colloquial	collateral

A somewhat smaller number of words begin with *col-*, among them:

colony	colonize	color
cologne	colonel	colossal
coliseum	colic	colon

10. com-, comm-.

Only memory and luck will help you to distinguish between these spellings. But one fact will help: many more words begin with *comm-* than with *com-*:

comedy	coma	comity
comet	comic	comestible
comatose	comedian	coming

command	commemorate	commend
commencement	comma	comment
commander	commercial	commission
commit	commune	committee
commentary	commiserate	commodore
common	communism	communicate

11. con-, conn-.

Before a vowel, the following are the only words of consequence spelled with *con-*:

cone	conical	conifer
conic	conundrum	coniferous

If a vowel does not follow this beginning, numerous words are spelled with *con-*:

concert	concern	concentrate
conception	concrete	conclude
confirm	confident	conflict
congregation	conquest	consent

If you are in doubt, double the *n* when the next letter is a vowel:

connect	connive	connective
connate	connivance	connoisseur
connote	connotation	connubial

12. cor-, corr-.

Before a vowel, *corr-* is more common than *cor-*:

correct	corridor	correlate
correspond	corrupt	corrosive
corrugate	corroborate	corrode
correctitude	correlative	corruption

The only *cor-* words that might be misspelled are:

coral	coronary	corollary
coronation	coroner	corespondent
cornice	cornucopia	corona

13. -cy, -sy.

When in doubt about ending a word having this sound, choose *-cy:*

fluency	lunacy	consistency
legacy	literacy	regency
infancy	frequency	sufficiency
constancy	democracy	secrecy

Note, however, that the *-sy* ending is needed in some words:

| jealousy | hypocrisy | heresy |
| idiosyncrasy | pleurisy | ecstasy |

14. dis-, diss-.

The addition of the prefix *dis-* to a word or word root beginning with *s* produces a "double *s*" pattern:

dissatisfy	dissident	disseminate
dissipate	dissimilar	dissociate
dissolve	dissonance	dissent
dissuade	dissolution	dissect

The addition of *dis-* to a word beginning with any letter other than *s* requires only one *s:*

disagree	disapprove	dispute
disappoint	displeasure	disqualify
disconnect	disprove	disquiet

15. -el, -ell.
    One-syllable words end in *-ell:*

tell	shell	well
bell	hell	fell
dell	sell	jell

Words of two or more syllables normally end in *-el:*

compel	rebel	excel
dispel	propel	expel
impel	repel	lapel
jewel	travel	parallel

16. en-, in-.
    Numerous English words start with the prefix *en-* or *in-* with no change in meaning. In these words, *en-* is preferred:

enrich	enchant	encounter
endorse	enthrone	enclose
endure	entitle	enclosure
entrap	enfold	encase
engulf	entrust	entomb

In the following words *in-* is preferred:

inquiry	ingrain	insurance
indoctrinate	insure	invoke
incorporate	infiltrate	inure

17. -ence, -ense.

Most words of more than one syllable end in *-ence* rather than *-ense:*

consequence	difference	experience
independence	sequence	affluence
impatience	eloquence	influence

Words ending in *-ense* include:

nonsense	defense	pretense
intense	condense	offense

18. -ension, -ention.

When faced with a choice between *-ension* and *-ention,* try to think of another form of the word being spelled. An *s* in that form suggests *-ension* (tense—tension), although exceptions are numerous. If the preceding letter is *h,* the ending is always *-ension* (apprehend-apprehension). If the preceding letter is *t,* the ending should be *-ention:*

comprehension	contention
tension	convention
suspension	distention
condescension	prevention
extension	retention
pretension	circumvention
dissension	intention

19. -eys, -ies, -ys.

Nouns that end in *ey* are usually pluralized by adding *s:*

alley—alleys	attorney—	monkey—
valley—valleys	attorneys	monkeys
key—keys	donkey—	
	donkeys	

Nouns that end in *y* preceded by a consonant are pluralized by changing *y* to *i* and adding *es:*

sky—skies	dairy—dairies	diary—diaries
fly—flies	spy—spies	delivery—
lady—ladies	soliloquy—	deliveries
story—stories	soliloquies	

If a proper noun ends in *y,* form the plural by adding *s:*

Harry—Harrys	Judy—Judys	Dorothy—
Jerry—Jerrys	Mary—Marys	Dorothys
Sally—Sallys		

20. fore-, for-.
    With one exception, *fore-* as the initial spelling of a word indicates a meaning of "before," or "earlier," or "front," or "previous," or "the front part of":

forearm	foreword	forehead
foretold	foreman	foreground
forecast	forefinger	forefather
forewoman	foremost	forenoon

The one exception is *foreclose* (*foreclosure*) which has none of the meanings mentioned.

Other words in which the prefix does not have any meaning of "early" or "before" or the like are spelled with *for-*:

forget	forward	forlorn
forgive	forbid	forbear
forsake	forfeit	forbearance
forgiveness	forgo	format

21. -k to -c.
    A verb ending in *-oke* has noun and adjective forms in which the *k* changes to *c* before the vowel *a:*

    convoke—convocation—convocable
    invoke—invocation—invocatory
    provoke—provocation—provocative
    evoke—evocation—evocative
    revoke—revocation—irrevocable

22. -ment.
    This suffix is added directly to a verb to form a noun:

develop—development	embarrass—embarrassment
equip—equipment	endanger—endangerment
assign—assignment	assess—assessment

Verbs ending in *e* form nouns without adding an additional
e:

manage—management	place—placement
entangle—entanglement	arrange—arrangement
amuse—amusement	state—statement

An often misspelled exception is "argue—argument." Also,
with verbs ending in *-dge* (judge, lodge, etc.) the preferred
spelling drops the final *e:* judgment, lodgment.

23. mis-, miss-.
The prefix *mis-* provides a negative force to a word:

conduct—misconduct	behave—misbehave
place—misplace	understand—misunderstand
apply—misapply	cast—miscast

When *mis-* is prefix to a word that starts with *s,* a double *s*
occurs:

shape—misshape	step—misstep
spell—misspell	speak—misspeak
state—misstate	spend—misspend

24. -ope, -oap.
Soap is the only common word ending in *-oap.* Other words
with this sound end in *-ope:*

antelope	scope	grope
mope	slope	dope
elope	hope	rope

25. -uous.
Don't omit the first *u* in the endings of these words:

arduous	virtuous	innocuous
strenuous	conspicuous	unctuous
superfluous	impetuous	continuous
contemptuous	tempestuous	ingenuous

16

TEST YOURSELF: THIRTY-FIVE GAMES AND QUIZZES

1. Insert *ei* or *ie* in the following:

ach_____ve	n_____ther
bel_____f	p_____ce
br_____f	perc_____ve
c_____ling	rec_____pt
conc_____t	rel_____ve
dec_____ve	rev_____w
for_____gn	sh_____ld
financ_____r	shr_____k
misch_____vous	v_____l
n_____ghbor	y_____ld

2. Insert *ei* or *ie* in the following:

cash_____r	rec_____ve
ch_____f	retr_____ve
f_____ld	s_____zure
fr_____ght	sh_____k
h_____nous	st_____n
h_____r	surv_____llance
h_____ght	th_____f
l_____sure	v_____n
p_____r	w_____ght
pr_____st	w_____rd

3. Add *-ed* and *-ing* to the following:

array	destroy	pity
copy	empty	pray
dally	imply	pry
delay	marry	rally
deny	pay	rely

| reply | stay | try |
| say | toy | typify |

4. Add *-ness* to each of the following:

bare	icy	pretty
busy	lively	shy
empty	lovely	wry
happy		

5. *Study—studies—studied—studying.* Supply the same verb forms for each of the following:

bury	enjoy	pity
carry	envy	pray
cry	marry	stay
dignify		

6. Add *-ing* and *-ment* to each of the following:

abridge	atone	judge
acknowledge	argue	move
advise	excite	settle
amuse		

7. Add *-ed* and *-ing* to each of the following:

acquit	occur	tax
admit	prefer	transfer
control	refer	transmit
infer		

8. The prefix *mis-* means "bad" or "wrong." It is found in many words such as *mistake, misnomer, misadvise, misinformation, mispronunciation, misrepresent, misgauge, misadventure, misbelief,* etc. First, write as many words as you can recall beginning with each of the following prefixes. Then expand your lists by reference to a good dictionary:

ad-	non-	pro-
de-	ob-	sub-
hyper-	poly-	ultra-
inter-		

9. By means of a suffix (*-ible* or *-able*, *-ly* or *-ally*, *-ence* or *-ance*, *-ion*, etc.) form an adjective, adverb, or noun from each of the following words. Example: *admire: admirable, admirably, admiration.* Not all these parts of speech can be formed from each word, but one or more can be:

accept	describe	love
advertise	detect	notice
allow	discern	remark
deduce		

10. Add *-ed* and either *-able* or *-ible* to the following:

avail	excite	reverse
comprehend	like	suggest
depend	presume	value
dismiss		

11. Add *-ally* or *-ly* to each of the following:

accident	incredible	occasion
complete	intention	physic
entire	lyric	true
incident		

12. From many verbs nouns may be formed which end in *-ance*, *-ence*, *-ar*, *-er*, *-or*; *-ary*, *-ery*. Example: *contribute, contributor.* Form a noun from each of the following words:

act	defer	protect
adhere	defy	provide
beg	distill (distil)	repent
carry	lecture	station
collect	lie	subsist
confer	occur	visit
counsel	prefer	

13. Form plurals of each of the following:

apparatus	bus	dynamo
area	cross-	elf
billiards	examination	hoof
bureau	dwarf	measles

metropolis   synopsis   thief
poet laureate   tactics   torpedo
quota

14. Some compounds are spelled as one word (*football*), some as hyphenated words (*four-dimensional*), some as two words (*reading desk*). Indicate the correct spelling of:

airtight   helterskelter   runin
boobytrap   highschool   schoolboy
campfire   inspite   selfstarter
chickenhearted   laborsaving   sodawater
downstairs   offstage   sunrise
drawbridge   pitchdark   twentyfour
hangeron   quietspoken

15. Supply the missing letter in each of the following:

ab_____ence   excell_____nt
absor_____tion   exigen_____y
apol_____gy   han_____kerchief
Ba_____tist   iden_____ity
caf_____teria   min_____ature
calend_____r   opt_____mistic
cem_____tery   sacr_____legious
compar_____tive   sep_____rate
disinfect_____nt   sim_____lar
dorm_____tory   temper_____ment

16. Supply the missing letter in each of the following:

appar_____nt   nes_____le
cors_____ge   priv_____lege
crim_____nal   p_____rsue
def_____nite   r_____diculous
friv_____lous   sacr_____fice
gramm_____r   su_____prise
ignor_____nt   tra_____edy
instruct_____r   tres_____le
irresist_____ble   vulg_____r
livel_____hood   We_____nesday

17. Some of the following words are correctly spelled, some incorrectly. Indicate which ones are which.

atheletic	height	reccommend
competition	mischieveous	safty
desireable	naturally	sulphur
discipline	obstacal	suppress
dissappointed	occassion	vengeance
embarassed	outragous	villain
environment	perseverance	

18. Which of the following are correctly spelled, which incorrectly?

alright	appelation	commited
analogous	changable	conscientious

Continue to indicate which of the following are correctly spelled, which incorrectly.

developement	paralel	scurrulous
ecstasy	pidgeon	symetrical
innoculate	questionaire	temperature
occasionally	renege	tendency
pantomime	rythmical	

19. Which of the following proper names are correctly spelled, which incorrectly?

Americian	Hawaian	Saturday
Britian	Kruschev	Tennesee
Brughel	Louisiana	Tripali
Burma	Massachusetts	Uraguay
Conneticut	Oragon	Wisconson
Edinburg	Phillipines	Worcestershire
February	Rockerfeller	

20. Consult your dictionary for the preferred or variant spellings of:

analyze	center	fulfil
armor	defense	instalment
canyon	dialogue	judgment
catalogue	esthetic	medieval

monologue	sulphur	traveler
savior	theatre	vigor
sextet	tranquillity	

21. The combining form *graph* appears in many English words. It comes from the Greek *graphos* (*graphein,* to write). Two examples are *telegraph,* "writing from a distance," and *monograph,* "writing on a single subject." Make a list of as many words as you can think of, or find in your dictionary, containing *graph* as a combining form.

22. The following is a list of everyday words with pronunciations as shown in reliable dictionaries. Spell each of them correctly:

WEBSTER'S NEW COLLEGIATE DICTIONARY	THE AMERICAN COLLEGE DICTIONARY	WEBSTER'S NEW WORLD DICTIONARY
ă · pēl′	ə pēl′	ə -pēl′
bĭz′nĕs	bĭz′nĭs	biz′nis
drī	drī	drī
ĕk · sĕl′	ik sĕl′	ik-sel′
kăl′ĕn · dẽr	kăl′ən dər	kal′ən-dẽr
kōld	kōld	kōld
nĕs′ĕ · sĕr′ĭ	nĕs′ə sĕr′i	nes′ə-ser′i
ôr′ĕnj	ôr′ĭnj	ôr′ənj
prŏ̄ · pōz′	prə pōz′	prə -pōz′
thûr′ō̄	thûr′ō̄	thũr′ō

23. Whether a good or bad speller, you will need to consult your dictionary frequently. You will lose time by not knowing the alphabet so thoroughly that you do not have to hesitate. Arrange the following words in the order in which they appear in a dictionary.

jump	radio
jean	read
jilt	refine
jerk	running
jiffy	risk
jeer	race
juvenile	round

jelly	rainfall
jeep	remain
join	red

24. Determine whether a study of the derivations of the following words will aid you in spelling them correctly:

absence	judicial
assign	language
bilious	mathematical
catercorner	pasteurize
criticism	possess
descend	research
emerald	ridiculous
foreign	shoulder
halitosis	typical
instrument	Wednesday

25. Using directions given in Exercise 21, list as many words as you can containing each of these combining forms:

electro-	phon-
forma-	-phone
para-	-ward

26. Correctly place apostrophes (only where needed) in the following:

> My mother-in-laws room
> My 5s are legible; yours look like ss.
> Hasnt he forgotten the troops uniforms?
> "Its theirs, not ours," Jack replied.
> He prefers Sophocles plays to Marxs tracts.
> King Edward VIIIs operation
> Thats somebody elses work, not hers.
> World War II (1939–45)
> Whos going to whose party tonight?
> You use too many *could be*s and *maybe*s.

27. Which word in each of the following pairs of words is spelled correctly? Find on pages 102–110 the spelling rule which applies.

achieve *or* acheive   carries *or* carrys
unnamed *or* unamed   fortieth *or* fortyeth
replacable *or* replaceable   thief *or* theif
amusement *or* amusment   mimicking *or* mimicing
photostatted *or* photostated   guideance *or* guidance

28. Using suggestions given on pages 118–119, devise a mnemonic for each of the *ten* words which give you the greatest spelling difficulty. Don't strain, but also don't worry if a mnemonic is quite bizarre: it's for your use only.

29. As pointed out several times in this book, studying lists of words difficult to spell is not really helpful. First, the only useful lists are of words which trouble you yourself. Second, most lists of "demons" contain words which are rarely used and which would stop even excellent spellers.

Here is a list of seventy-five troublesome words, most or all of which you might use. Choose the correct (or preferred) spelling from the two columns. A score of sixty or more qualifies you as a superior speller.

1.	absence	abscence
2.	accidently	accidentally
3.	accomodate	accommodate
4.	acheive	achieve
5.	acknowledgment	acknowledgement
6.	acquaintance	aquaintance
7.	allotted	alloted
8.	analize	analyze
9.	anoint	annoint
10.	arguement	argument
11.	assistant	assisstant
12.	bankruptcy	bankrupcy
13.	basically	basicly
14.	benefited	benefitted
15.	changable	changeable
16.	commission	commision
17.	commitee	committee
18.	connoiseur	connoisseur
19.	conscientious	conscientous

20.	defenseless	defenceless
21.	dilettante	dilletante
22.	disappoint	disapoint
23.	disasterous	disastrous
24.	dissatisfied	disatisfied
25.	dissipate	disippate
26.	drunkenness	drunkeness
27.	embarrassment	embarassment
28.	encouragment	encouragement
29.	exhiliration	exhilaration
30.	familiar	familar
31.	fascinating	facinating
32.	Febuary	February
33.	genealogy	geneology
34.	goverment	government
35.	harrass	harass
36.	hypocrisy	hypocricy
37.	incidently	incidentally
38.	innoculate	inoculate
39.	iridescent	irridescent
40.	labortory	laboratory
41.	leisurely	liesurely
42.	loneliness	lonliness
43.	neice	niece
44.	nineth	ninth
45.	noticeable	noticable
46.	occurence	occurrence
47.	optomistic	optimistic
48.	pamphlet	pamplet
49.	permissable	permissible
50.	picnicking	picnicing
51.	practicly	practically
52.	preparation	preperation
53.	pronounciation	pronounciation
54.	puntuation	punctuation
55.	recommend	reccommend
56.	restaurant	restarant
57.	scarsity	scarcity
58.	seize	sieze

59. siege	seige
60. superstiton	superstition
61. supprised	surprised
62. temperament	temperment
63. tradegy	tragedy
64. truly	truely
65. tyrany	tyranny
66. ukelele	ukulele
67. unforgetable	unforgettable
68. unnecessary	unecessary
69. vacilate	vacillate
70. villianous	villainous
71. Wednesday	Wensday
72. weight	wieght
73. weird	wierd
74. wield	weild
75. yeild	yield

30. You are an above-average speller if you can score 75 or more on the following list of 100 words which range from "trouble makers" to outright "demons." Master them. Then try them on your friends—and your enemies.

1. academy	17. collaborate	33. fulfilled
2. accessory	18. consensus	34. garage
3. accumulate	19. corollary	35. *Gesundheit*
4. acoustics	20. dahlia	36. gnome
5. alimentary	21. defendant	37. haughty
6. aloha	22. desiccated	38. hearse
7. anonymity	23. dilapidated	39. homogeneous
8. apparatus	24. disastrous	40. impromptu
9. attendant	25. eleemosynary	41. innuendo
10. avoirdupois	26. emphatically	42. irreducible
11. baccalaureate	27. eulogy	43. irrelevant
12. bullion	28. exaggerate	44. jeopardize
13. buoy	29. exercise	45. knapsack
14. bureaucracy	30. facile	46. labyrinth
15. cantankerous	31. fascinate	47. larynx
16. catechism	32. frantically	48. licorice

49. liqueur	67. pseudo	84. thermometer
50. mediocre	68. psychiatry	85. tonsillitis
51. millennium	69. queue	86. tranquil
52. moratorium	70. quinine	87. turgid
53. naphtha	71. rarefied	88. ultimatum
54. negotiable	72. rehearsal	89. umbrella
55. notarize	73. rendezvous	90. uterus
56. octogenarian	74. reservoir	91. vice versa
57. orchid	75. rheumatic	92. vitamin
58. overrun	76. saxophone	93. vulnerable
59. paralysis	77. schedule	94. wharf
60. perennial	78. seismograph	95. wiener
61. pharmaceutical	79. separation	96. wrestle
62. phosphorus	80. sieve	97. xylophone
63. phrenology	81. silhouette	98. yeast
64. phylactery	82. spontaneity	99. zinnia
65. poinsettia	83. surveillance	100. zoological
66. precinct		

31. Fix in your mind the spelling of these medical terms by discovering how they are formed with the aid of combining forms, prefixes, and suffixes:

anesthesiology	ophthalmology
cardiovascular	orthopedics
endocrinology	otolaryngology
gastroenterology	pathology
hematology	pediatrics
neurology	psychiatry
obstetrics	radiology
oncology	urology

32. The game Doublets is played by altering one word into another through changing one letter at a time, each step resulting in a new word. Here's how to change *four* to *five:*

> four—foul—fool—foot—fort—fore—fire—five

Change each of the following:

chin into *nose*	*poor* into *rich*
tears into *smile*	*winter* into *summer*

33. Choose the correctly spelled word in each of the following
    pairs:

absurd—abserd	humorous—humerous
across—acros	occassion—occasion
alright—all right	omitted—omited
condemn—condem	lonliness—loneliness
convenient—convenent	remittance—remitance
criticise—criticize	resistable—resistible
daily—daley	separate—seperate
dependant—dependent	tacitun—taciturn
develope—develop	tolorate—tolerate
existence—existance	woolen—woollen

34. Here is a list of words, some of them relatively new, that are
    being increasingly used. Fix their meanings and their spellings
    so as to be up-to-date in your word usage.

aerobic	fusion	quantum
algorithm	gentrification	quark
astrodome	geodesis	quasar
astrophysics	helix	replication
bioelectricity	heterodynamics	retrovirus
cellulose	hydrospace	rodenticide
cloning	laser	semiconductor
cognitive	mach	silicon
cryogenics	microwave	subatomic
diabetologist	oceanography	supernova
dioxin	ordnance	theodolite
electronics	polymer	ultrasound
extraterrestrial	pseudopods	unicellular

35. In each group of three words below, one may be misspelled.
    Find the misspelled word; then decide which rule, if any,
    applies to it. In the space at the left, write a letter to
    indicate that the correct spelling of the word falls under the
    rule treating: a—*ei* or *ie,* according to preceding letter and
    pronunciation of the vowels; b—final *e* or final *y* when a
    suffix is added; c—doubling the final consonant (or not) when
    a suffix is added; d—exceptional spelling required to preserve

the pronunciation of the word; e—none of these: the correct spelling of the word is contrary to rule.

1. conceive
   drooping
   changable
2. neighbor
   benefited
   sieze
3. briefing
   writing
   layed
4. beleiving
   looted
   lovable
5. annoyance
   alloted
   extremely

6. likelyhood
   weighing
   fighting
7. grievous
   forgetable
   happiness
8. kercheif
   reference
   meanness
9. canceled
   noticable
   luckily
10. leaving
    ladylike
    developed

GLOSSARY:
TERMS USED IN THIS BOOK

Any useful book on spelling must use expressions that may be unfamiliar to you but are closely tied to the spelling problem. Below you will find brief definitions or explanations of several linguistic terms. Some of these are fully defined in the book itself; others are used or implied. When studying the book itself, refer to this glossary if you come across an expression that you do not fully understand. An effort has been made to include all terms likely to need clarification. If you are still in doubt, consult your dictionary.

accent: Accent is the emphasis given to a letter or syllable or word when speaking it. This increased force results from stress, or pitch, or both. In dictionaries, marks are used to show the placing and kind of emphasis required. For example, in the word *envelop* the second syllable is accented: en vel' op. In *envelope,* the first syllable has primary stress, or accent: en' vel ope. See *stress,* below.

adjective: An adjective modifies a noun or pronoun by describing, limiting, or in some other closely related way making meaning more nearly exact. An adjective may indicate quality or quantity, may identify or set limits. Adjectives are therefore of three general types: descriptive (a *red* hat, a *hard* lesson, a *damaged* thumb); limiting (the *fourth* period, her *former* home, *many* times); proper (an *American* play, a *Colorado* melon).

Some adjectives—indeed, most— have endings that mark them as adjectives. The more important of these include:

> *-y:* rocky, funny, dreamy, fussy, muddy
> *-ful:* harmful, faithful, hurtful, sinful
> *-less:* stainless, timeless, lawless, guiltless
> *-en:* golden, wooden, given, hidden, rotten
> *-able (-ible):* favorable, desirable, credible
> *-ive:* obtrusive, submissive, impulsive
> *-ous:* amorous, ridiculous, generous, marvelous

-ish: womanish, selfish, Danish, fortyish
-al: cordial, optional, experimental, judicial
-ic: metric, philosophic, authentic, artistic
-ary: primary, visionary, contrary, secondary
-some: meddlesome, tiresome, handsome, troublesome

An adjective may modify a noun directly ("this *yellow* light thrown upon the color of his ambitions") or indirectly ("the survivors, *weary* and *emaciated,* moved feebly toward the ship"). In sentences such as "The water felt *cold*" and "The corn is *ripe,*" each adjective is related to the subject, the word it modifies, by a linking verb. (A linking verb has little meaning of its own; it functions primarily as a connection between subject and predicate noun or predicate adjective.) In the sentences above, *cold* and *ripe* are called *predicate adjectives* or complements.

adverb: An adverb modifies a verb, adjective, or other adverb by describing or limiting to make meaning more exact. Adverbs usually tell *how, when, where, why, how often,* or *how much.* In "A low cry came *faintly* to our ears," the adverb modifies the verb *came.* In "Close the door *very* softly," the adverb modifies the adverb *softly.*

Adverbs have the following characteristics: (1) They are commonly, but not always, distinguished from corresponding adjectives by the suffix *-ly: bad, badly; sure, surely; cold, coldly.* (2) Certain adverbs are distinguished from corresponding nouns by the suffixes *-wise* and *-ways: endways, sideways, lengthwise.* (3) Certain adverbs are distinguished from corresponding prepositions in not being connected to a following noun: "He ran *up*" (adverb); "he ran *up* the street" (preposition). (4) Like adjectives, but unlike nouns and verbs, adverbs may be preceded by words of the *very* group (intensifiers): "The *most exotically* dressed girl passed by"; "he went *right* by."

base word: Any word, or part of a word which is a combining form, to which may be added prefixes, suffixes, etc. Thus we refer to *mortal* as the base word, or element, of *mortality* and *cede* as the base element of the word *accede.* See *root word,* below.

capitals: Any letters written or printed in a form larger than, and often different from, that of corresponding small letters: A, B, C; a, b, c. The use of capital letters (sometimes called upper-case letters as contrasted with small, or lower-case, letters) is discussed in Chapter 10.

clause: A group of words which forms a sentence or a part of a sentence. A clause contains a subject (substantive) and a predicate (verb). "*John studied* and *I played the radio*" illustrates two separate and independent clauses. In the following sentence, the first group of italicized words is an independent clause, the second is dependent upon the first: "*I shall telephone you/when I arrive.*"

compounds: Compound words are combinations of two or more words: *doorkeeper, inasmuch as.* The use of hyphens (see below) with compound words is discussed in Chapter 9.

conjunction: A part of speech which serves as a linking or joining word to connect words or groups of words such as phrases and clauses: *and, but, for, because, since,* etc.

consonant: A consonant is a speech sound produced by restricting or stopping the breath. Consonants may be contrasted with *vowels* (see below) since the latter involve sounds made with less friction and fuller resonance. The consonants *b, d, g, k, p,* and *t* are produced by stopping and releasing the air stream. The consonants *l, m, n,* and *r* are produced by stopping the air stream at one point while it escapes at another. In sounding the consonants *f, s, v,* and *z,* the air stream is forced through a loosely closed or narrow passage. In short, consonants are those letters (sounds) of the alphabet which are not vowels: *a, e, i, o, u.*

diacritical mark: A mark added to a letter to indicate pronunciation by giving it a particular sound (phonetic) value or stress which distinguishes it from an unmarked letter of similar form. Thus the sound we utter in starting the alphabet may be indicated as $\bar{a}$, as in the words *date* and *able.* The sound of *a* in *art* and *father* is represented by $\ddot{a}$. Every dictionary worthy of the name devotes considerable space to its own system of diacritical marks, usually running a condensed list of them on the bottom of each righthand page and a detailed explanation inside the front or back cover or in pages at the front of the dictionary. Diacritical marks are essential to correct pronunciation and thus are important in learning to spell correctly. You should become thoroughly familiar with the marks used by your dictionary.

etymology: The branch of linguistic study which deals with the origin and development of words. For further discussion see Chapter 5.

grammar: Grammar is ordinarily understood as a series of statements of the way a language works; English grammar is "the English way of saying things." That is, grammar concerns the form of words; their use in phrases, clauses, and sentences; their tenses, cases, and other changes in form. The word *grammar,* which comes from the Greek word *gramma* ("letter," "written symbol"), now means the structure of an entire given language.

Thus defined, grammar is unconcerned with what is "correct" or "incorrect," "right" or "wrong." However, there *is* so-called prescriptive grammar. This kind has to do with the application of "rules" as guides to expression.

homograph: A word with the same spelling as another but with a different origin and meaning: a *bow* tie, to bend a *bow; row,* meaning a noisy dispute and a straight line; *fair,* meaning "beautiful" and also "a market"; *lead,* the metal and a word meaning "to conduct"; *air,* "atmosphere" and "a melody"; *pale,* an "enclosure" and "faintly colored." See Chapter 3 for further discussion.

homonym: A word with the same pronunciation as another but with a different origin, meaning, and sometimes spelling: *hear, here; steal, steel; meat, meet; pale, pail.* For further discussion, see Chapter 3.

hyphen: A mark used between the syllables of a divided word or the parts of a compound word. It is more a mark of spelling than of punctuation. See Chapter 9.

long sound: A pronounced vowel or consonant which is held or sounded for a relatively long time. For example, the *a* in *ape* is long; it may be held for as long as your breath lasts. In dictionaries it is marked $\bar{a}$. Similarly, the *e* in *easy* is long; the *i* in *mile,* etc.

morpheme: A term in linguistics for the smallest meaningful unit in an utterance. A morpheme may be a single phoneme (such as the article "a"), a prefix or suffix ("ad-," "-ism"), a single syllable or several ("girl," "instructor," "miscellaneous").

morphology: The patterns of word formation in language, including derivation and inflection. Morphology and syntax together form a basic division of grammar.

noun: A noun (derived from the Latin word *nomen,* meaning "name") designates or names a person, place, or thing; a quality, idea, or action; an event or point in time. This less than really helpful definition can be supplemented by consideration of the ways in which nouns are characterized and classified. Nouns are usually preceded by such words as *the, a, an, my, your, his, her, some, each, every, their, this, that.*

Certain nouns have characteristic endings (*-al, -tion, -ness, -ment, -ure, -dom, -ism, -ance,* for example) that distinguish them from corresponding verbs or adjectives: *arrive, arrival; determine, determination; depart, departure; real, realism; rely, reliance; wise, wisdom.*

Nouns and identically spelled verbs may sometimes be differentiated by accent. The first member in each of these pairs of words is a noun, the second a verb: *per' mit, permit'; rec'ord, record'; sur'vey, survey'; ob' ject, object'.*

Nouns are found in set positions, such as before a verb (a *mouse* roars), after a verb (wash the *shirt*), or after a preposition (working for *money*).

Nouns may be singular or plural in number. The plural of most English nouns is obtained by adding *s* or *es* to the singular form: *girls, books, trees, fields, peaches.* Some nouns have only one form for both the singular and the plural: *deer, sheep, moose.* Some nouns have irregular plurals: *oxen, children, mice.* Some actually have no plurals: *fun, furniture.*

Nouns have three genders: (1) masculine (*man, boy*), (2) feminine (*girl, woman*), and (3) neuter (*chalk, earth*). When a noun may be either masculine or feminine, it has a common gender (*teacher, friend*).

Nouns have three cases: nominative (subject), objective, and genitive (possessive). In English, nouns have a common form for both the nominative and the objective case. An apostrophe is used to designate a noun in the genitive case: *Jack's, boat's, neighbor's.*

A *common* noun is a name given to all members of a class: *dozen, infant, farm, street, city, boy, structure.* Common nouns may be recognized as such because they do *not* begin with a capital letter (except at the beginning of a sentence or as part of a name).

A *proper* noun names a particular member of a class: it *does* begin with a capital: *Rover, Michael, Twin Cedars, Roosevelt Freeway, Atlanta, Bob Dylan, Eiffel Tower.*

An *abstract* noun is the name of a quality or general idea that cannot be known directly by the senses: *faith, happiness, courage, fear.*

Concrete nouns name material (tangible) things that can be perceived by one or more of the senses: *fire, aroma, notebook, hamburger, stone, record, cake.*

A *collective* noun names a group of individuals. Although it refers to more than one, it is singular in form: *pair, committee, squad, team, crowd, crew, assembly.*

orthography: This is a ten-dollar word to indicate what this book is all about. It means, simply, correct spelling, or spelling as a science.

particle: This is an omnibus word, a convenient catchall which includes short and indeclinable parts of speech such as articles, prepositions, conjunctions, and interjections, as well as prefixes and suffixes. These are particles: *but, oh, in, ad-, -ion.*

parts of speech: The classifications to which every word must belong: noun, pronoun, adjective, adverb, verb, preposition, conjunction, interjection. The same word may belong to several parts of speech depending upon how it is used in a sentence.

person: The change in the form of a pronoun or verb—sometimes, merely a change in use as with verbs—to indicate whether the "person" used is the person speaking (first person), the person spoken to (second person), or the person or thing spoken about (third person): *I* read, *you* read, *he* reads.

phoneme: The smallest meaningful unit of *sound* in a language. The letters in our alphabet comprise about forty phonemes. For example, the word *wean* consists of three phonemes: w, $\bar{e}$, and n. Compare with *morpheme,* above.

phonetics: The branch of language study dealing with speech sounds, their production and combination, and their representation by symbols.

phrase: A group of related words not containing a subject (substantive) and predicate (verb). It may contain from two to twenty words but is always a part of a sentence and is never independent: *was running, having finished my typing, my work done, out into the cold night,* etc.

plural number: A classification of nouns, pronouns, etc., to indicate two or more units or members. *Singular* number is the classification to indicate one. For further discussion, see Chapter 7.

prefix: A syllable, group of syllables, or word united with or joined to the beginning of another word to alter its meaning or to create a new word. *Pre-* itself is a prefix in *preheat* (to heat beforehand). For further discussion, see Chapter 6.

preposition: A part of speech showing the relationship of a noun or pronoun to some other word: *at* the office, *across* the street. The word literally means "placed before": "pre-position."

pronoun: A part of speech which is used instead of a noun, primarily to avoid repetition and prevent overuse of the noun. The word *pronoun* consists of *pro,* meaning "for" or "instead of," plus *noun.*

pronunciation: The art or manner of uttering words with reference to the production of sounds, accent, etc. Pronunciation is complex and many-faceted; it involves, among other things, levels of pronunciation, dialect, provincialisms, and, most importantly, spelling. For further discussion, see Chapter 4.

root word: A base, a morpheme, to which prefixes, suffixes, etc., may be added. See *base word* and *morpheme,* above.

short sound: Sounds which are relatively brief in duration. See *consonant* and *long sound,* above. Many letters of the alphabet are sounded with short duration or stress and in varying degrees. Contrast the long *a* in *hate* with the short *a* in *hat,* for only one of many examples of short sounds.

sibilants: A hissing sound or the symbol for it. *S, sh, z, zh, ch,* and *j* are sibilants: *pressure, shirt, zero,* etc.

singular number: See *plural number,* above.

stress: The relative force with which a syllable is uttered. In English there are primary (strong) stress; secondary (light) stress; zero (silent) stress. See *accent,* above, and Chapter 4.

substantive: An inclusive term for a noun, pronoun, phrase or clause used as a noun, and for a verbal noun. The only practical value of the word *substantive* is that its use avoids repeating all the words used in this definition. Like most catchalls, it is a somewhat loose term.

suffix: A sound, syllable, or syllables added at the end of a word or word base to change its meaning, alter its grammatical function, or form a new word: *dark,* dark*ness.* See *prefix,* above.

syllable: A word or part of a word, usually the latter, pronounced with a single, uninterrupted sounding of the voice. Note the syllables in these words: *sec re tar y* (4 syllables); *fun ny* (2 syllables); *fa mil iar i za tion* (6 syllables).

syntax: The arrangement of words in a sentence to show their relationship. Briefly, it may be identified as *sentence structure* and is not an especially helpful term.

tense: The time of the action or of the state being expressed by the verb. The three simple, or primary, tenses are *present, past,* and *future.* The three compound, or secondary, tenses are *present perfect, past perfect, future perfect.*

verb: A part of speech expressing action or a state of being: "The river *flows,*" "I *am* here."

vowel: A speech sound articulated so that there is a clear channel for the voice through the middle of the mouth. Grammatically, the vowels in English are *a, e, i, o, u* and, in some instances, *w* and *y.* See *consonant,* above.

-Able, -ible, 65–70
Ac-, acc-, 138
-Acious, -aceous, -atious, 138
Ad-, 63
Added vowels, 48
Af-, aff-, 139
Ag-, agg-, 139
All-, al-, 139
-Ally, -ly, 70–71
American Heritage Dictionary, 57
-Ance, -ence, 71–72
Anglo-Saxon language, 5
Ante-, anti-, 63
Ap-, app-, 140
Apostrophe, 86–89
-Ar, -er, -or, 72–74
-Ard, -ards, 140
-Ary, -ery, 74
Auditory image, 13
-Ayed, -aid, 140

Beginning and endings of words, 138–46
Borrowing of words, 5–6

Capital letters, 96–100
Carelessness in spelling, 111–16
Caxton, William, 7
-Cede, -ceed, -sede, 74–75
-Ceed, 74–75
Chaucer, Geoffrey, 6
Col-, coll-, 141
Com-, comm-, 141
Combining forms, 78–80
Compound nouns, 83–84

Compound words, 90–95
Con-, conn-, 141–42
Consonants:
    doubled, 107–109
    dropped, 50–51
Cor-, corr-, 142
-Cy, -sy, 142

De-, dis-, 64
Derivation of words, 56–60
Dictionary:
    apostrophe and, 86–89
    capitalization and, 96–100
    choice of, 57
    combining words and, 78–80
    compound words and, 90–95
    etymology and, 56–60
    plurals and, 81–85
    prefixes and, 61–65
    suffixes and, 65–78
    use of, 61–100
Dictionary-makers, 7
Dis-, diss-, 142–43
Doubling final consonant, 107–109
Dropped consonants, 50–51

-Efy, -ify, 75
-Ei, -ie, 102–103
-El, -ell, 143
En-, in-, 143
-Ence, -ance, 71–72
-Ence, -ense, 144
-Ension, -ention, 144
-Er, 72–74
-Ery, -ary, 74

Etymology, 56–60
-Eys, -ies, -ys, 144

Final consonant, doubled, 107–109
Final consonant rule, 107–109
Final *e,* 105–107
Final *y,* 104–105
Fore-, for-, 145
Foreign nouns, plural of, 84–85
*Funk and Wagnalls Standard College
    Dictionary,* 57

Games of spelling, 11, 147–59
Glossary of spelling terms, 161–68
-Graph, 61

Homographs, 18
Homonyms, 18–19
Hyphen, 90–95

-Ible, -able, 65–70
-Ie, -ei words, 102–103
-Ify, -efy, 75
Images:
    auditory, 13
    mental, 13
    motor, 13–14
    visual, 16–42
Inserted *k,* 107
Inter-, 64
Irregular plurals, 84
-Ise, -ize, -yze, 75–78

Jackson, Andrew, quoted, 3–4
Johnson, Samuel, 7
    paraphrased, 57

-K to *-c,* 145
Letters, silent, 53–56
Listing misspelled words, 122–37
Look-alikes, 19–42
-Ly, 70–71

Memory devices, 117–21
-Ment, 145–46

Mental images, 13
Mis-, miss-, 146
Mispronunciation, 45–46
Misspelled words, list of, 123–37
Mnemonics, 117–21
Motor image, 13–14

Norman conquest, 5
Nouns:
    compound, 83–84
    foreign, 84–85
    plural of, 81–85
    possessive case of, 86–89
Noun plurals, 81–85

Old English, 5
"One plus one" rule, 109–10
-Ope, -oap, 146
-Or, 72–74

Perception span, 17–19, 112–14
Plurals, 81–85
Poetry, capitalization of, 98
Possessive case, 86–89
Prefixes and suffixes, 61–78
    incorrect, 47–48
Pronouns, possessive of, 86–89
Pronunciation, 43–55
Proofreading, 112–14
Proper nouns, capitalization of,
    97–98

Quizzes in spelling, 147–59

*Random House Dictionary of the
    English Language,* 57
Rules for spelling, 101–10

-Sede, 74–75
Schwa, 51–52
Seeing words, 16–42
Shakespeare, 6
Silent letters, 53–56
Sound-alikes, 19–42
Sound systems in dictionaries, 44
Span of vision, 113–14

Spelling:
  carelessness and, 111–16
  comforting thoughts about, 8–11
  development of, 3–8
  difficulty of, 3–4
  games of, 11, 147–59
  history of, 4–8
  memory devices for, 117–21
  plurals and, 81–85
  pronunciation and, 43–55
  rules for, 101–10
  terms used in, 161–68
Spelling lists, value of, 122–23
Suffixes, 65–78

Terms used in spelling, defined,
  161–68
Tests in spelling, 147–59
Titles, capitalization of, 98
Troublesome beginnings, endings,
  138–46
Twenty most often misspelled words,
  123–24

Un-, 64–65
Unstressed vowels, 51–53
-Uous, 146

Veblen, Thorstein, quoted, 3
Vision spread, 113–14
Visual images, 16–42
Visualizing words, 16–42
Vowels:
  added, 48
  dropped, 48–49
  unstressed, 51–53

Webster, Noah, 7
Webster's New Collegiate Dictionary,
  57
Webster's New World Dictionary of
  the American Language, 57
Word derivation, 56–60
Word joining, principles of, 90–91

-Yze, 75–78